Top 100 Mos

Dumpling Recipes

A Dumpling Cookbook

by Graham Bourdain

Copyright Page

Top 100 Most Delicious Dumpling Recipes

Copyright © 2024 by Graham Bourdain

All rights reserved. No part of this publication may be reproduced, distributed, or transmitted in any form or by any means, including photocopying, recording, or other electronic or mechanical methods, without the prior written permission of the publisher, except in the case of brief quotations embodied in critical reviews and certain other noncommercial uses permitted by copyright law.

First Edition

Disclaimer

The information in "Top 100 Most Delicious Dumpling Recipes" is for general information purposes only. The author and publisher make no representation or warranties with respect to the accuracy, applicability, fitness, or completeness of the contents of this book. They disclaim any warranties (expressed or implied), merchantability, or fitness for any particular purpose.

The author and publisher shall in no event be held liable for any loss or other damages, including but not limited to special, incidental, consequential, or other damages. As always, the advice of a competent legal, tax, accounting, or other professional should be sought.

The author and publisher do not warrant the performance, effectiveness, or applicability of any sites listed or linked to in this book. All links are for information purposes only and are not warranted for content, accuracy, or any other implied or explicit purpose.

Note: Cooking times and temperatures, ingredient measurements, and instructions mentioned in this book are guidelines only. Variances in cooking appliances, altitudes, climates, and individual techniques may necessitate adjustments in preparation. Always use your best judgment and test recipes in small batches where possible.

Table of Contents

Asian Dumplings

1. Pork and Chive Dumplings 10
2. Shrimp Shumai 12
3. Chicken Siu Mai 14
4. Tibetan Momo 18
5. Korean Kimchi Manda 20
6. Char Siu Bao 22
7. Crystal Har Gow 24
8. Mushroom and Tofu Potstickers 26
9. Vegetarian Gyozas 30
10. Cantonese Wontons 32

European Dumplings

11. German Potato Dumplings (Kartoffelknödel) 34
12. Hungarian Chicken Paprikash Dumplings 36
13. Polish Peirogi (Potato & Cheese) 38
14. Italian Ricotta Gnudi 40
15. Austrian Speckknödel 42
16. Slovakian Bryndzové Halušky 44
17. Czech Bread Dumplings 46
18. Russian Pelmini 48
19. Swedish Kroppkaka 50
20. French Quenelles 52

North American Dumplings

21. Southern Chicken and Dumplings 54
22. Apple Dumplings 56
23. Drop Biscuit Dumplings 58
24. Matzoh Ball Soup Dumplings 60
25. Cornmeal Dumplings 62

South American Dumplings

26. Brazilian Coxinha 64
27. Argentine Empanadas 66
28. Colombian Arepas. 68
29. Bolivian Salteñas 70

African Dumplings

30. Moroccan Chicken Pastilla 72
31. South African Steak Bunny Chow 74
32. Nigerian Moi Moi (Bean Dumplings) 76
33. Kenyan Ugali 78

Indian Subcontinent

34. Potato & Pea Dumplings 80
35. Paneer Momo 82
36. Lentil Dumpling (Dahi Vada) 84
37. Malabar Chicken Paratha 86
38. Gujiya (Sweet Dumplings) 88

Middle Eastern Dumplings

39. Turkish Manti (Lamb Dumplings) 90

40. Kurdish Kubbeh... 92

41. Persian Gondhi (Chicken Chickpea Dumplings) 94

Oceanian Dumplings

42. Australian Meat Pie Dumplings 96

43. New Zealand Seafood Pie 98

Dessert Dumplings

44. Chocolate & Cherry Dumplings..100

45. Mango & Sticky Rice Dumplings 102

46. Red Bean Bao 104

47. Sweet Ricotta Dumplings with Raspberry Sauce 106

48. Plum Dumplings (Szilvásgombóc) 108

49. Coconut Dumplings 110

50. Fried Banana Dumplings 112

51. Nutella and Marshmallow Dumplings 114

52. Blueberry Pierogi 116

53. Almond and Orange Blossom Dumplings.......................................118

Vegetarian & Vegan Dumplings

54. Spinach and Ricotta Dumplings 120

55. Edamame & Truffle Dumplings 122

56. Vegan Jackfruit 'Pork' Dumplings 124

57. Cauliflower and Potato Samosas 126

58. Vegan Lentil and Mushroom Dumplings 128

59. Sweet Potato and Black Bean Empanadas 130

60. Zucchini & Corn Dumplings 132

Seafood Dumplings

61. Lobster & Corn Dumplings 134

62. Tuna Tartare Potstickers 136

63. Scallop & Chive Dumplings 138

64. Crab Rangoon 140

65. Fish and Dill Pierogi 142

Meat Dumplings

66. Lamb and Rosemary Dumplings 144

67. Beef Bourguignon Dumplings 146

68. Turkey & Sage Dumplings 148

69. Duck and Hoisin Dumplings 150

Breakfast Dumplings

70. Bacon, Egg, and Cheese Bao 152

71. Sausage and Maple Syrup Dumplings 154

72. Blueberry Pancake Dumplings 156

73. Cinnamon Roll Dumplings 158

Fusion Dumplings

74. Pizza Dumplings 160

75. Tandoori Chicken Bao 162

76. Taco Empanada Dumplings 164

77. Thai Green Curry Chicken Dumplings................................ 166

Gluten-Free Dumplings

78. Quinoa and Vegetable Dumplings 168

79. Gluten-Free Prawn Har Gow 170

80. Gluten-Free Chicken & Herb Dumplings 172

Dairy-Free Dumplings

81. Dairy-Free Spinach and Pine Nut Dumplings................... 174

82. Dairy-Free Shrimp & Cilantro Dumplings 176

Spicy Dumplings

83. Spicy Beef & Szechuan Pepper Dumplings 178

84. Spicy Tofu & Kimchi Dumplings 180

Soup Dumplings

85. Xiao Long Bao (Pork Soup Dumplings) 182

86. Beef Broth & Onion Soup Dumplings............................... 184

87. Tomato Soup & Grilled Cheese Dumplings 186

Cold Dumplings

88. Cold Peanut Noodle Dumplings 188

89. Cold Cucumber & Dill Dumplings..................................... 190

Raw Dumplings

90. Raw Vegan Fruit Dumplings 192

91. Raw Zucchini & Cashew Dumplings 194

Unique & Experimental

92. Beet & Goat Cheese Dumplings 196

93. Pumpkin & Sage Dumplings 198

94. Coffee & Cream Dumplings 200

95. Pecan Pie Dumplings 202

96. Matcha & White Chocolate Dumplings 204

97. Bourbon & Bacon Dumplings 206

98. Roasted Red Pepper & Feta Dumplings 208

99. Wasabi & Tuna Dumplings 210

100. Popcorn Chicken Dumpling Pockets 212

Bonus recipes for Dumpling dough 214

Review Request 217

1. Pork and Chive Dumplings

Alright, folks, we're diving into the world of Pork and Chive Dumplings – a classic that's as fun to make as it is to eat. Imagine the sizzle as they hit the pan, the steam as they cook, and that first, heavenly bite. It's a journey through flavor town, and you're the driver. Let's get our hands dirty and our stomachs ready!

Prep: 60 min. Cook: 10 min. Ready in: 1 h 10 min. Servings: 4

Ingredients:

For the Dough:

2 cups all-purpose flour

3/4 cup boiling water

For the Filling:

1 pound ground pork

1 cup chives, finely chopped

2 tablespoons soy sauce

1 tablespoon sesame oil

1 tablespoon grated ginger

2 cloves garlic, minced

1 teaspoon sugar

Salt and pepper, to taste

For Cooking:

Vegetable oil

Water

Cooking Directions:

Let's start with the dough. It's simpler than you think. In a large bowl, slowly mix the boiling water into your flour. Stir it with a fork until it starts to come together. When it's cool enough, get your hands in there and knead it on a floured surface. You're going for a smooth, elastic dough. Let it rest under a damp cloth for about 30 minutes. It's like giving the dough a little spa time.

While the dough is resting, let's get that filling ready. In a bowl, mix your ground pork, chives, soy sauce, sesame oil, ginger, garlic, sugar, and a good pinch of salt and pepper. Mix it well – don't be shy. Get in there with your hands. It's all about getting those flavors to know each other.

Roll out your dough on a floured surface until it's thin. We're talking about the thickness of a nickel. Use a cookie cutter or a glass to cut out circles. Now, spoon a small amount of filling into the center of each circle. Fold them over into half-moons and pinch the edges to seal. It's like tucking in a delicious little pork and chive blanket.

Heat a little oil in a pan over medium heat. Place the dumplings in, but don't overcrowd them. They need their personal space. Cook until the bottom is golden brown – it's all about that crunch. Then, add a splash of water and cover. Let them steam for about 5 minutes or until the pork is cooked through and the dough is tender.

Uncover, let any remaining water evaporate, and get those beauties onto a plate. Serve them with your favorite dipping sauce. It's a journey from crispy bottom to tender, juicy top – a perfect dumpling experience.

And there you have it, my culinary comrades, Pork and Chive Dumplings. It's a dance of textures and flavors, a true testament to the art of dumpling-making. Remember, cooking is about exploration, mistakes, and, most importantly, having a good time. So enjoy your creation, share it with friends, or hoard them all for yourself (I won't judge). Until next time, keep those taste buds adventurous and your kitchen full of laughter. Bon appétit!

Enjoy

2. Shrimp Shumai

Alright, we're about to dive into the world of Shrimp Shumai. Picture this: a steaming bamboo steamer, opening to reveal these little parcels of joy. It's like each Shumai is whispering, "Eat me, I'm delicious." This isn't just food; it's a culinary adventure in a small, steamed package. Let's make some magic happen in your kitchen.

Prep: 60 min. Cook: 10 min. Ready In: 1 h 10 min. Servings: 4

Ingredients:

For the Dough:

2 cups all-purpose flour

3/4 cup boiling water

For the Filling:

1 pound shrimp, peeled, deveined, and finely chopped

1/4 cup water chestnuts, finely chopped

2 green onions, finely chopped

1 tablespoon soy sauce

1 teaspoon sesame oil

1/2 teaspoon grated ginger

1 clove garlic, minced

Salt and pepper, to taste

For Cooking:

Carrot slices or peas for garnish (optional)

Cooking Directions:

Begin your culinary journey with the dough. In a large mixing bowl, slowly add boiling water to the flour while stirring continuously. When the mixture starts coming together, transfer it to a floured surface. Knead it until it's smooth and elastic – think of it as a mini workout for your hands. Cover the dough with a damp cloth and let it rest for about 30 minutes. This rest is as crucial for the dough as it is for a good steak.

While the dough rests, combine your finely chopped shrimp, water chestnuts, green onions, soy sauce, sesame oil, ginger, garlic, and a dash of salt and pepper in a bowl. Mix them until they're well acquainted.

After its rest, roll out your dough on a lightly floured surface. Aim for thinness – you should almost be able to see your hand through it. Use a round cutter or a glass to cut out circles for your Shumai wrappers.

Place a spoonful of the shrimp mixture in the center of each wrapper. Now, here's the fun part: bring the dough up around the filling, creating a little "open-top" package. It should look like a tiny cupcake. Top each with a slice of carrot or a pea if you're feeling fancy. Arrange your Shumai in a steamer lined with parchment paper or cabbage leaves, making sure they don't touch. Cover and steam for about 10 minutes. You're looking for the shrimp to be pink and smiling at you, saying, "I'm done!"

Serve these steamed beauties hot. They're little bites of heaven, perfect as they are, but a dipping sauce can add an extra layer of flavor.

And voilà, your homemade Shrimp Shumai is ready to impress. You've just brought a piece of the dim sum experience into your home. Each bite is a testament to your culinary skills and the magic that happens when you put time and love into your cooking. Remember, every dish tells a story, and this Shumai is your narrative. So share it, savor it, and most importantly, enjoy the journey. Happy cooking!

Enjoy

3. Chicken Siu Mai

Today's culinary escapade brings us to Chicken Siu Mai, a twist on a dim sum classic. Imagine yourself in the heart of Hong Kong's vibrant food scene, each Siu Mai a bite of tradition and innovation. We're not just cooking here; we're creating a masterpiece that's as pleasurable to make as it is to eat. Let's get the steam rising and flavors mingling!

Prep: 60 min. Cook: 10 min. Ready in: 1 h 10 min. Servings: 4

Ingredients:

For the Dough:

2 cups all-purpose flour

3/4 cup boiling water

For the Filling:

1 pound ground chicken

1/4 cup shiitake mushrooms, finely chopped

1/4 cup water chestnuts, finely chopped

2 green onions, finely chopped

1 tablespoon soy sauce

1 teaspoon sesame oil

1/2 teaspoon grated ginger

1 clove garlic, minced

Salt and pepper, to taste

For Cooking:

Carrot slices or peas for garnish (optional)

Cooking Directions:

Begin with the dough – mix the boiling water gradually into the flour, stirring continuously. When it starts to form a rough dough, transfer it to a floured surface and knead until smooth and elastic. Let this dough rest under a damp cloth for about 30 minutes, giving it time to develop the perfect texture.

While the dough is resting, take this time to prepare the filling. Combine the finely chopped cabbage, grated carrot, chopped shiitake mushrooms, green onion, soy sauce, sesame oil, ginger, and garlic in a bowl. Season it with salt and pepper. The key here is to get a nice balance of flavors and textures – each ingredient plays its part in the overall symphony of taste. Once the dough is ready, roll it out on a lightly floured surface. You're aiming for thinness here, so roll it until it's just a few millimeters thick. Use a round cutter to cut out circles for your Gyoza wrappers.

Now comes the fun part – assembling the Gyozas. Place a small spoonful of your vegetable filling in the center of each wrapper. Then, fold the wrapper over the filling to create a half-moon shape, pinching the edges to seal. Imagine you're creating little crescents of joy – each one a bite-sized delight.

To cook your Gyozas, heat some vegetable oil in a pan over medium heat. Place the dumplings in the pan and cook until the bottoms are golden brown – that's where the magic happens, giving you that delightful crunch. Then, add a splash of water to the pan and cover it. Let them steam for about 5 minutes or until the wrappers are tender and the filling is cooked through.

Serve your Vegetarian Gyozas hot, with a side of soy sauce or your favorite dipping sauce. They're perfect for sharing, but you might want to keep them all to yourself – and that's okay too.

There you have it, a plate of homemade Vegetarian Gyozas, each one a testament to your culinary skills and creativity. This dish is more than just a meal; it's a journey through the flavors of Japan, right from the comfort of your kitchen. Remember, cooking is an adventure, and every adventure is worth sharing. So, invite your friends, gather your family, and enjoy these little parcels of joy together. Until next time, keep exploring the world through your taste buds!

Enjoy

4. Tibetan Momo

Embark on a culinary expedition to the heart of the Himalayas with Tibetan Momos. These dumplings are more than just a staple in Tibetan cuisine; they're a cultural icon, a symbol of warmth and hospitality in a land known for its mystical beauty. Making Momos is not just about cooking; it's about connecting with a rich, ancient culture. Let's bring a piece of Tibetan tradition into your kitchen and onto your plate.

Prep: 25 min. Cook: 30 min. Ready in: 55 min. Servings: 4

Ingredients:

For the Dough:

2 cups all-purpose flour

3/4 cup water (room temperature)

For the Filling:

1 pound ground beef or yak meat (traditional, if available)

1 onion, finely chopped

1/2 cup cilantro, finely chopped

1 teaspoon minced garlic

1 teaspoon minced ginger

1 teaspoon ground cumin

1/2 teaspoon turmeric

Salt and pepper, to taste

Cooking Directions:

Start with the dough. In a large bowl, mix the flour with room-temperature water to form a soft, pliable dough. Knead it on a floured surface until it's smooth – think of it as a meditative process, bringing you closer to the heart of Tibetan cooking. Cover the dough and let it rest for about 30 minutes.

While the dough is resting, let's get the filling ready. Combine the ground beef or yak meat, onion, cilantro, garlic, ginger, cumin, turmeric, salt, and pepper in a bowl. Mix it well – you want the flavors to meld together, creating a harmonious blend that's both earthy and aromatic.

Now, roll out the dough on a floured surface until it's about 2mm thick. Use a round cutter to cut out circles. These will form the base of your Momos.

Place a spoonful of the meat filling in the center of each dough circle. The art of Momo-making is in the folding – pinch and pleat the edges, gathering them at the top. It should look like a small, pleated pouch – each Momo a testament to your craftsmanship.

To cook the Momos, steam them in a steamer lined with cabbage leaves or parchment paper for about 10 minutes. They're done when the dough is firm, and the filling is cooked through.

Serve your Tibetan Momos hot, accompanied by a spicy tomato chutney or a simple soy sauce. It's a journey through taste and tradition with every bite.

Congratulations, you've just created a little piece of Tibet in your own kitchen. Momos are more than a meal; they're a story, a journey, a connection to a land rich in culture and history. Share these with friends and family and take pride in the tradition you've brought to your table. Until our next culinary adventure, keep exploring the world one dumpling at a time!

Enjoy

5. Korean Kimchi Manda

Get ready to spice up your dumpling game with Korean Kimchi Mandu. These dumplings are a celebration of flavors and textures, a testament to Korea's rich culinary heritage. Making Kimchi Mandu is like composing a symphony – each ingredient plays a crucial role, creating a harmonious blend that's both bold and satisfying. Let's embark on this flavorful journey and bring a piece of Korea to your dining table.

Prep: 1 h 30 min. Cook: 10 min. Ready In: 1 h. 40 min. Servings: 4

Ingredients:

For the Dough:

2 cups all-purpose flour
3/4 cup water (room temperature)

For the Filling:

1 cup kimchi, finely chopped and squeezed dry
1/2 pound ground pork or beef
1/4 cup tofu, mashed
1/4 cup glass noodles, soaked in hot water and chopped
1 green onion, finely chopped
1 teaspoon sesame oil
1 teaspoon soy sauce
1/2 teaspoon sugar
1 garlic clove, minced
Salt and pepper, to taste

Cooking Directions:

The journey begins with the dough. In a bowl, mix the flour and room-temperature water to form a smooth dough. Knead it on a floured surface until it's elastic and soft. Cover it and let it take a little rest – about 30 minutes should do. As the dough rests, turn your attention to the heart of this dish – the filling. Combine the finely chopped and squeezed kimchi, ground pork or beef, mashed tofu, chopped glass noodles, green onion, sesame oil, soy sauce, sugar, minced garlic, salt, and pepper in a mixing bowl. This is where the magic happens, where flavors meld and come to life. Now, roll out the rested dough on a floured surface until it's thin. You're aiming for a thickness that's just right to hold the filling but thin enough to ensure a delicate bite. Cut out circles using a round cutter. Place a spoonful of the kimchi filling onto the center of each dough circle. Folding Mandu requires a bit of technique – fold the dough over the filling and seal the edges, creating a half-moon shape. Feel free to add pleats for a traditional look, or keep it simple – it's your masterpiece, after all. To cook the Mandu, you have options: steam, boil, or pan-fry. For steaming, place them in a steamer for about 10 minutes until cooked through. For boiling, drop them into boiling water until they float to the surface. And for pan-frying, fry them in a little oil until crisp and golden brown on each side. Serve your Korean Kimchi Mandu hot, with a dipping sauce made of soy sauce and a drop of sesame oil. It's a burst of Korea in every bite, a perfect blend of tangy, savory, and umami flavors.

There you have it – a plate of delicious Korean Kimchi Mandu, each dumpling a small bite of joy. These aren't just dumplings; they're a culinary journey, a way to explore new flavors and traditions right in your own kitchen. Share them with friends and family, or enjoy them all by yourself – either way, you've created something special. Keep experimenting, keep tasting, and most importantly, keep enjoying the art of cooking. Until our next culinary escapade, happy cooking!

Enjoy

6. Char Siu Bao

Imagine the bustling streets of Hong Kong, the scent of fresh dim sum wafting through the air. That's where we're going with Char Siu Bao. These fluffy buns filled with sweet and savory BBQ pork are a cornerstone of Cantonese cuisine. Making Char Siu Bao at home is like taking a culinary trip to the heart of Hong Kong. So let's roll up our sleeves and bring this delightful street food experience to your kitchen.

Prep: 2 h. Cook: 20 min. Ready in: 2 h. 20 min. Servings: 4

Ingredients:

For the Dough:

2 1/2 cups all-purpose flour
1/4 cup sugar
1/2 teaspoon salt
1 tablespoon baking powder
1 tablespoon active dry yeast
1 cup warm water
2 tablespoons vegetable oil

For the Char Siu Filling:

1 cup char siu (Chinese BBQ pork), diced
1 tablespoon vegetable oil
2 garlic cloves, minced
2 tablespoons oyster sauce
2 tablespoons hoisin sauce
1 tablespoon soy sauce
1 tablespoon sugar
1 tablespoon cornstarch
2 tablespoons water

Cooking Directions:

Begin with the dough. In a large bowl, combine flour, sugar, salt, and baking powder. In a separate bowl, dissolve the yeast in warm water and let it sit until it's frothy – about 10 minutes. Combine the yeast mixture with the dry ingredients, add the vegetable oil, and mix until a dough forms. Knead the dough on a floured surface until it's smooth and elastic. Place it in a greased bowl, cover with a damp cloth, and let it rise in a warm place until it doubles in size – about 1 hour.

While the dough is doing its magic, prepare the char siu filling. Heat the vegetable oil in a pan, add the minced garlic, and stir-fry until fragrant. Add the diced char siu, oyster sauce, hoisin sauce, soy sauce, and sugar. Mix the cornstarch with water and add it to the pan, stirring constantly until the sauce thickens. Let the filling cool completely – it's the heart of your Char Siu Bao.

After the dough has risen, punch it down and divide it into small equal-sized pieces. Roll each piece into a ball, then flatten each ball into a circle. Place a spoonful of the char siu filling in the center of each circle. Gather the edges of the dough and pinch them together at the top to seal. It's like wrapping a precious gift – the char siu filling nestled cozily inside.

Steam the buns in a bamboo steamer over boiling water for about 20 minutes, until they are puffed up and soft. The transformation is almost magical – from a simple dough to a pillowy bun filled with rich, savory flavors.

Serve the Char Siu Bao hot, straight from the steamer. Each bite takes you on a journey through the flavors of Cantonese cooking – the sweetness of the pork, the richness of the sauces, and the softness of the bun.

And there you have it, your very own homemade Char Siu Bao. This dish is more than just a dumpling; it's a cultural experience, a taste of the vibrant streets of Hong Kong. Whether you're sharing them with family or enjoying them solo, these buns are sure to bring a smile to your face. Keep exploring the vast world of dumplings, and remember, each recipe is a new adventure. Happy cooking, and enjoy your delicious creation!

Enjoy

7. Crystal Har Gow

Welcome to the delicate world of Crystal Har Gow, where the art of dim sum takes center stage. These elegant dumplings, with their glistening, crystal-like wrappers, are a testament to the finesse of Cantonese cuisine. Making Har Gow is like performing a delicate dance with dough and filling, a process that's both meditative and rewarding. Let's bring this dim sum staple to life in your kitchen.

Prep: 1 h. 30 min. Cook: 10 min. Ready in: 40 min. Servings: 4

Ingredients:

For the Dough:

1 cup wheat starch

1/2 cup tapioca starch

1 cup boiling water

1 tablespoon vegetable oil

For the Filling:

1 pound shrimp, peeled, deveined, and finely chopped

1 tablespoon bamboo shoots, finely chopped (optional)

1 green onion, finely chopped

1 teaspoon grated ginger

1 tablespoon soy sauce

1 teaspoon sesame oil

1 teaspoon sugar

Salt and white pepper, to taste

Cooking Directions:

The dough is the star in Har Gow. Start by mixing wheat starch and tapioca starch in a bowl. Carefully pour in the boiling water while stirring vigorously. Add the vegetable oil and mix until a dough starts to form. When it's cool enough to handle, knead it until smooth. This dough is a bit more delicate than your average dough, so handle it with care. Let it rest while you prepare the filling.

For the filling, combine the finely chopped shrimp, bamboo shoots (if using), green onion, grated ginger, soy sauce, sesame oil, sugar, salt, and white pepper. This mixture should be fragrant and flavorful, with each ingredient playing its part.

Now, back to the dough. Roll it out on a lightly floured surface until it's thin, but not too thin – it needs to hold the filling without tearing. Cut out circles using a small round cutter.

Place a small amount of the shrimp filling in the center of each dough circle. The art of Har Gow is in the pleating – carefully pleat the edges of the dough, sealing the filling inside. It should look like a little purse or a crescent moon.

Steam the Har Gow in a bamboo steamer lined with parchment paper for about 10 minutes. They're ready when the dough becomes translucent, and the shrimp filling is cooked through.

Serve your Crystal Har Gow hot, straight from the steamer. They're best enjoyed with a side of soy sauce or a chili dipping sauce. Each bite is a mix of the delicate dough and the juicy, flavorful shrimp – a true dim sum delight.

Congratulations on mastering the art of Crystal Har Gow! These dumplings are not just a dish; they're a celebration of skill and flavor, a journey through the heart of Cantonese dim sum. Share them with friends and family or savor them yourself as a special treat. Remember, the journey of cooking is about exploring new techniques and flavors, one delicious bite at a time. Happy cooking and enjoy your culinary creation!

Enjoy

8. Mushroom and Tofu Potstickers

We're diving into the world of Mushroom and Tofu Potstickers, a vegetarian twist on a classic Asian dumpling. This recipe is a celebration of flavors and textures – the umami of mushrooms, the richness of tofu, all wrapped up in a crispy, golden-brown shell. Making potstickers is like creating little pockets of joy – let's get started and bring these delightful dumplings to your table.

Prep: 1 h. Cook: 15 min. Ready in: 1 h. 15 min. Servings: 4

Ingredients:

For the Dough:

2 cups all-purpose flour
3/4 cup boiling water

For the Filling:

1 cup shiitake mushrooms, finely chopped
1/2 cup firm tofu, crumbled
1 carrot, grated
2 green onions, finely chopped
1 tablespoon soy sauce
1 teaspoon sesame oil
1 clove garlic, minced
1 teaspoon grated ginger
Salt and pepper, to taste

For Cooking:

Vegetable oil

Cooking Directions:

Begin with the dough. In a large mixing bowl, pour the boiling water into the flour, stirring continuously. When the mixture begins to come together, transfer it to a floured surface and knead until smooth. This is your canvas – a simple dough that'll transform into crispy, golden potstickers. Let it rest under a damp cloth for about 30 minutes.

While the dough is resting, let's prepare the filling. In a bowl, mix together the finely chopped shiitake mushrooms, crumbled tofu, grated carrot, green onions, soy sauce, sesame oil, minced garlic, grated ginger, salt, and pepper. It's a melody of flavors that perfectly complements each other, creating a harmonious filling for your potstickers.

Roll out the rested dough on a floured surface until it's thin. Cut out circles using a round cutter – these are the wrappers for your potstickers.

Place a small amount of the mushroom and tofu filling in the center of each wrapper. Fold the dough over the filling to create a half-moon shape, and crimp the edges to seal. It's like wrapping up a tiny, edible present.

Heat a bit of vegetable oil in a pan over medium heat. Carefully place the potstickers in the pan, flat side down. You're looking for that sizzle – the sound of the dough starting to crisp up. Fry them until the bottoms are golden brown, then add a splash of water and cover the pan. The steam will cook the tops of the potstickers, making the wrapper tender while keeping the bottom crispy.

After a few minutes, remove the lid and let any remaining water evaporate. Give the potstickers a little shake to ensure they're not sticking, and then transfer them to a serving plate. They should have a beautiful contrast – crispy on the bottom, tender on the top.

Serve your Mushroom and Tofu Potstickers hot, with a dipping sauce made of equal parts soy sauce and rice vinegar, and a drop of sesame oil if you like. It's a simple sauce, but it complements the potstickers perfectly, adding a little acidity and sweetness to the savory filling.

There you have it, a plate of Mushroom and Tofu Potstickers, each one a perfect little bite of flavor and texture. These dumplings are a testament to the beauty of vegetarian cooking – simple ingredients coming together to create something truly special. Whether you're a vegetarian or just looking to try something new, these potstickers are sure to satisfy. Remember, cooking is an adventure – embrace the process, enjoy the flavors, and share your creations with the people you love. Happy cooking, and enjoy your delicious potstickers!

Enjoy

9. Vegetarian Gyozas

Enter the world of Vegetarian Gyozas, where every bite is a celebration of fresh, vibrant flavors. These dumplings are a testament to the fact that vegetarian food can be just as satisfying and flavorful as any meat-based dish. We're about to turn simple vegetables into something extraordinary. So, grab your apron and let's get started on this culinary journey.

Prep: 1 h. Cook: 10 min. Ready in: 1 h. 10 min. Servings: 4

Ingredients:

For the Dough:

2 cups all-purpose flour
3/4 cup boiling water

For the Filling:

2 cups cabbage, finely chopped
1 carrot, grated
1/2 cup shiitake mushrooms, finely chopped
1 green onion, finely chopped
1 tablespoon soy sauce
1 teaspoon sesame oil
1/2 teaspoon grated ginger
1 clove garlic, minced
Salt and pepper, to taste

For Cooking:

Vegetable oil
Water

Cooking Directions:

Start with the dough by mixing the boiling water into the flour. Stir until it begins to form a rough dough. Transfer it to a floured surface and knead until smooth. This is your blank canvas, ready to be filled with a delicious concoction. Let it rest under a damp cloth for about 30 minutes.

For the filling, mix together the chopped cabbage, grated carrot, shiitake mushrooms, green onion, soy sauce, sesame oil, ginger, garlic, salt, and pepper in a bowl. The mix of vegetables should be aromatic and inviting, a mélange of nature's best.

Roll out the rested dough on a floured surface until thin. Use a round cutter to cut out circles for your Gyoza wrappers.

To assemble, place a small spoonful of your vegetable filling in the center of each wrapper. Fold the dough over the filling to create a half-moon shape, pinching the edges to seal. You're crafting little pockets of joy, each one a testament to your culinary skills.

To cook, heat some vegetable oil in a pan over medium heat. Place the Gyozas in the pan and cook until the bottoms are golden brown – a delightful crunch awaits. Add a splash of water and cover the pan, allowing the steam to cook the tops, making the wrappers tender.

Serve the Gyozas hot, with a dipping sauce of your choice. The crisp exterior and the juicy, flavorful interior make for a perfect bite.

And there you have it – your very own homemade Vegetarian Gyozas. These dumplings are more than just a meal; they are a journey through flavors and textures. Whether you're a seasoned vegetarian or just exploring meat-free options, these Gyozas are sure to delight. Remember, cooking is an exploration – of ingredients, techniques, and flavors. Share your creations, enjoy the process, and let your culinary imagination soar. Happy cooking!

Enjoy

10. Cantonese Wontons

Let's transport your kitchen to the bustling streets of Guangzhou with Cantonese Wontons. These little morsels are a staple in Cantonese cuisine, offering a delightful combination of tender meat and shrimp encased in a silky wrapper. Wonton making is an art form, a balance of texture and flavor, where every fold holds a piece of tradition. Ready to dive in?

Prep: 1 h. Cook: 5 min. Ready in: 1 h. 5 min. Servings: 4

Ingredients:

For the Filling:

1/2 pound ground pork
1/4 pound shrimp, peeled, deveined, and minced
1 green onion, finely chopped
1 teaspoon grated ginger
1 tablespoon soy sauce
1 teaspoon sesame oil
1/2 teaspoon sugar
Salt and white pepper, to taste

For the Wontons:

Wonton wrappers
For the Soup (Optional):
4 cups chicken broth
2 green onions, sliced
A few leaves of bok choy or spinach
Salt and white pepper, to taste

Cooking Directions:

Begin by preparing the filling. In a bowl, mix together ground pork, minced shrimp, chopped green onion, grated ginger, soy sauce, sesame oil, sugar, salt, and white pepper. This is where flavor meets harmony – each ingredient complementing the other, ready to be encased in a delicate wrapper.

Take a wonton wrapper and place a small amount of the filling in the center. Moisten the edges of the wrapper with water – this is your glue. Fold the wrapper over the filling to form a triangle, pressing the edges to seal. Then, bring the two opposite corners together and press them to create a little parcel of deliciousness.

If you're opting for wonton soup, prepare the broth by bringing chicken broth to a gentle simmer. Add sliced green onions, bok choy or spinach, and season with salt and white pepper. Keep it simple – the broth is a comforting backdrop to the wontons, not the main act.

To cook the wontons, bring a pot of water to a boil. Add the wontons and cook for about 5 minutes, or until they float to the surface and the filling is cooked through. The transformation is beautiful – the wrappers become translucent, revealing the succulent filling inside.

Serve the wontons either in the broth or on their own, with a dipping sauce on the side. Each bite is a journey through Cantonese culinary history – a mix of succulent meat, tender shrimp, and delicate dough.

And there you have it – Cantonese Wontons, a dish steeped in history and flavor. Whether enjoyed in a comforting bowl of soup or as a standalone delicacy, these wontons are sure to bring warmth and joy to your table. Cooking is about more than just feeding the body; it's about nourishing the soul. Share these with loved ones and revel in the joy of homemade goodness. Until next time, happy cooking!

Enjoy

11. German Potato Dumplings (Kartoffelknödel)

Imagine a cozy German kitchen, the heart of the home, where the comforting scent of potato dumplings is wafting through the air. Kartoffelknödel, as they are known in Germany, are more than just a side dish; they're a warm hug on a plate, a culinary embodiment of comfort. These dumplings are simple yet satisfying, a perfect example of the wholesome and hearty nature of German cooking. Let's bring this comfort to your kitchen.

Prep: 1 h. 30 min. Cook: 20 min. Ready in: 1 h. 50 min. Servings: 4

Ingredients:

2 pounds potatoes, preferably starchy variety

1/4 cup all-purpose flour, plus more for dusting

2 tablespoons cornstarch

1 large egg

Salt and nutmeg, to taste

Bread crumbs (optional, for filling)

Butter (optional, for filling)

Oil for frying and sautéing

Cooking Directions:

Start by boiling the potatoes in their skins until they are tender. This is where patience pays off – the potatoes need to be just right. Once they're cooked, drain them and let them cool until they're easy to handle. Then, peel the potatoes and mash them until smooth. This is your dumpling base, the foundation of a good Kartoffelknödel.

In a large bowl, mix the mashed potatoes, flour, cornstarch, and egg. Season with salt and a pinch of nutmeg. If you're feeling adventurous, add a bit of bread crumbs and a cube of butter in the center of each dumpling for a surprise filling. Knead the mixture until it forms a smooth dough. It should be firm enough to hold its shape but still tender – a delicate balance.

Bring a large pot of salted water to a gentle simmer. While the water is heating, form the potato mixture into balls. Dust your hands with flour to prevent sticking – you're sculpting edible art here.

Carefully lower the dumplings into the simmering water. This is not a race; take your time. Let them cook for about 15-20 minutes. They're done when they float to the surface, a sign they're ready to be enjoyed. Serve the Kartoffelknödel as a side to a rich meat dish, or enjoy them as they are, perhaps with a drizzle of melted butter or a savory sauce. Each dumpling should be a soft, pillowy bite of comfort, a taste of home.

Imagine a cozy German kitchen, the heart of the home, where the comforting scent of potato dumplings is wafting through the air. Kartoffelknödel, as they are known in Germany, are more than just a side dish; they're a warm hug on a plate, a culinary embodiment of comfort. These dumplings are simple yet satisfying, a perfect example of the wholesome and hearty nature of German cooking. Let's bring this comfort to your kitchen.

Enjoy

12. Hungarian Chicken Paprikash Dumplings

Let's bring the heartwarming flavors of Hungary into your kitchen with Chicken Paprikash Dumplings. This dish is a testament to the comfort and depth of Hungarian cooking, where each spoonful is a warm embrace of flavors. Chicken Paprikash, with its rich and smoky paprika sauce, combined with soft, pillowy dumplings, creates a meal that's both satisfying and heartening. So, tie on your apron, and let's create a dish that's steeped in tradition and taste.

Prep: 1 h. Cook: 30 min. Ready in: 1 h. 30 min. Servings: 4

Ingredients:

For the Chicken Paprikash:

2 tablespoons vegetable oil
4 chicken thighs, bone-in and skin-on
2 onions, finely chopped
2 garlic cloves, minced
2 tablespoons sweet paprika
1 cup chicken broth
1 cup sour cream
Salt and pepper, to taste

For the Dumplings:

2 cups all-purpose flour
4 eggs
1/2 cup water
Salt, to taste

Cooking Directions:

Begin by heating vegetable oil in a large pot over medium heat. Season the chicken thighs with salt and pepper and brown them on both sides. You're not just cooking chicken here; you're building layers of flavor. Once browned, remove the chicken and set it aside.

In the same pot, add the onions and garlic, cooking until the onions are soft and translucent. Now, for the star of the show – the paprika. Add it to the onions and stir until they're coated and the aroma fills your kitchen. Return the chicken to the pot, add chicken broth, and bring it to a simmer. Cover and let it cook until the chicken is tender, infusing the broth with its flavors.

While the chicken is simmering, make the dumplings. In a bowl, mix together flour, eggs, water, and a pinch of salt to form a thick, sticky dough. This dough is the heart of the dish, so give it some love.

Bring a pot of salted water to a boil. Using two spoons or a small ice cream scoop, form the dough into small dumplings and drop them into the boiling water. They're ready when they float to the surface, light and ready to soak up the sauce.

Once the chicken is cooked, gently remove it from the pot. Stir in the sour cream to the paprika sauce, adjusting the seasoning as needed. Add the dumplings to the sauce, letting them bask in the creamy, smoky goodness.

Serve the Chicken Paprikash Dumplings hot. Each bite should be a perfect blend of tender chicken, rich sauce, and soft dumplings – a true taste of Hungary.

And there you have Hungarian Chicken Paprikash Dumplings, a dish that's not just a meal, but a culinary journey. It's a comforting, flavorful embrace that showcases the depth and warmth of Hungarian cuisine. Share this dish with loved ones, and enjoy the stories and connections that unfold around your table. Until we cook again, enjoy every bite and the memories you create along the way. Jó étvágyat!

Enjoy

13. Polish Peirogi (Potato & Cheese)

Today, we're embarking on a culinary journey to Poland with their iconic Pierogi. These little dumplings are a labor of love, a comfort food that has been passed down through generations. Filled with a simple yet satisfying mixture of potatoes and cheese, and encased in a tender dough, Pierogi are a true celebration of Polish culinary traditions. So, let's roll up our sleeves and bring a taste of Poland to your kitchen.

Prep: 1 h. 30 min. Cook: 5 min. Ready in: 1 h. 35 min. Servings: 4

Ingredients:

For the Dough:

2 cups all-purpose flour

1/2 cup water

1 egg

1/2 teaspoon salt

For the Filling:

2 large potatoes, peeled and cubed

1 cup farmer's cheese or ricotta cheese

1 onion, finely chopped

2 tablespoons butter

Salt and pepper, to taste

Cooking Directions:

Begin with the dough. In a large bowl, mix together the flour, water, egg, and salt. Knead the mixture on a floured surface until the dough is smooth and elastic. It's the vessel that will carry the flavorful filling, so give it the attention it deserves. Let it rest for about 30 minutes.

Meanwhile, for the filling, boil the potatoes until they are soft and mashable. In a separate pan, sauté the finely chopped onion in butter until it's golden and soft. Combine the mashed potatoes, sautéed onion, and cheese in a bowl. Season with salt and pepper. This filling should be creamy, rich, and full of flavor.

Once the dough has rested, roll it out on a floured surface until it's thin, but not too thin – it needs to hold the filling securely. Use a round cutter or a glass to cut out circles.

Place a spoonful of the potato and cheese filling onto each dough circle. Fold the dough over, creating a half-moon shape, and press the edges to seal. Ensure they're well sealed so the filling stays cozily inside during cooking.

Bring a large pot of salted water to a boil. Add the Pierogi in batches, being careful not to overcrowd the pot. They cook quickly – in about 5 minutes or when they float to the surface. For a different texture, you can also pan-fry the boiled Pierogi in butter until they are crisp and golden.

Serve the Pierogi hot, with a dollop of sour cream or extra sautéed onions on top. Each bite is a delightful combination of creamy filling and tender dough, a dish that's both humble and deeply satisfying.

And there you have it, Polish Potato & Cheese Pierogi, a dish that brings the heart and soul of Polish cooking to your table. Whether you're celebrating a family tradition or trying something new, Pierogi are a delicious way to explore the rich tapestry of European cuisine. Enjoy the process, share your creations, and, as always, savor every bite. Smacznego!

Enjoy

14. Italian Ricotta Gnudi

Embark on a culinary journey to the heart of Tuscany with Italian Ricotta Gnudi. These dumplings are a celebration of simplicity and flavor, where the creamy texture of ricotta takes center stage. Gnudi, which means 'naked' in Italian, are often described as ravioli without the pasta coating – a pure expression of the filling's delicate flavors. Let's bring this simple yet elegant dish to your kitchen and indulge in the essence of Italian cooking.

Prep: 60 min. Cook: 5 min. Ready in: 1 h. 5 min. Servings: 4

Ingredients:

1 1/2 cups ricotta cheese

1/2 cup grated Parmesan cheese

2 eggs, lightly beaten

1 cup spinach, cooked, drained, and chopped (optional)

1/2 cup all-purpose flour, plus more for dusting

Salt and nutmeg, to taste

Your choice of sauce for serving (e.g., sage butter or marinara)

Cooking Directions:

Start by mixing the ricotta cheese, Parmesan, beaten eggs, and chopped spinach (if using) in a bowl. Season this mixture with salt and a hint of nutmeg. The spinach adds a lovely color and a subtle earthy flavor, but it's optional. Add the flour to the mixture, gently folding it in to form a soft, pliable dough. The trick here is to be gentle – overworking the dough can make the Gnudi dense.

Let the dough rest for about 30 minutes. This resting time allows the flour to hydrate and the flavors to meld together.

Bring a large pot of salted water to a gentle boil. While waiting, shape the dough into small, walnut-sized balls. Lightly dust your hands and the Gnudi with flour to prevent sticking. This shaping process is where you connect with the food – each Gnudi is a little piece of art.

Gently drop the Gnudi into the boiling water. They cook quickly, usually in about 3-5 minutes. You'll know they're ready when they float to the surface, a sign they are perfectly cooked and ready to be savored.

Serve the Gnudi hot with your choice of sauce. A simple sage butter sauce can highlight their delicate flavor, while a rich marinara sauce can add a robust, heartier touch.

And there you have it – Italian Ricotta Gnudi, a dish that's as comforting as it is elegant. These dumplings are a testament to the beauty of Italian cuisine, where a few quality ingredients come together to create something truly special. Enjoy these light, fluffy pillows of ricotta goodness with friends and family, and savor the joy of Italian cooking. Buon appetito!

Enjoy

15. Austrian Speckknödel

Today, we're stepping into the world of Austrian comfort food with Speckknödel. This dish is a cozy embrace in the form of dumplings, combining the rustic charm of bread with the rich flavor of speck. Speckknödel are versatile and beloved in Austrian kitchens, often enjoyed in a savory broth or alongside a fresh salad. It's a culinary journey to the Alps, where every bite resonates with tradition and comfort.

Prep: 45 min. Cook: 20 min. Ready in: 1 h. 5 min. Servings: 4

Ingredients:

2 cups bread cubes (preferably day-old bread)

1/2 cup milk

1/4 cup speck or bacon, finely chopped

1 small onion, finely chopped

2 tablespoons butter

2 eggs

1/4 cup all-purpose flour

2 tablespoons fresh parsley, chopped

Salt and pepper, to taste

Nutmeg, to taste

Chicken or beef broth (for serving, optional)

Cooking Directions:

Begin by soaking the bread cubes in milk until they're soft but not mushy. This is the base of your dumplings, offering a wonderful texture and the ability to absorb flavors beautifully.

In a skillet, melt the butter and sauté the chopped onion and speck until the onion is translucent and the speck is slightly crispy. This step infuses the butter with a smoky, savory flavor that will permeate the dumplings.

In a mixing bowl, combine the soaked bread cubes, the sautéed onion and speck, eggs, flour, parsley, and season with salt, pepper, and a touch of nutmeg. Mix everything until well combined. The mixture should be moist but firm enough to shape into dumplings.

Bring a large pot of salted water or broth to a gentle simmer. While it's heating, form the mixture into medium-sized balls, roughly the size of a golf ball.

Carefully lower the dumplings into the simmering water or broth. Let them cook for about 15-20 minutes. They should rise to the surface and be firm to the touch.

Serve the Speckknödel hot, either in a bowl of broth as a light meal or as an accompaniment to a hearty stew or salad. They're a wonderful combination of the comforting texture of bread dumplings and the rich, smoky flavor of speck.

And there you have it, Austrian Speckknödel, a dish that's as hearty as it is comforting. Whether you're nestled in the mountains of Austria or in your own home, these dumplings bring a taste of Alpine tradition to your table. Enjoy the warmth and depth of flavors, and as always, share the joy of cooking with those you love. Guten Appetit!

Enjoy

16. Slovakian Bryndzové Halušky

Today, we're diving into the heart of Slovakian cuisine with Bryndzové Halušky. This dish is a celebration of simple, hearty ingredients coming together to create a comforting and satisfying meal. The combination of soft, pillowy dumplings, tangy bryndza cheese, and crispy bacon offers a delightful contrast in textures and flavors. It's a rustic dish that speaks of tradition and home cooking at its finest. Let's bring a taste of Slovakia to your table.

Prep: 60 min. Cook: 20 min. Ready in: 1 h. 20 min. Servings: 4

Ingredients:

For the Halušky (Dumplings):

4 large potatoes, peeled and grated
1 1/2 cups all-purpose flour
1 egg
Salt, to taste

For the Topping:

1 cup bryndza cheese (or another soft sheep's cheese, or a mixture of feta and cream cheese as a substitute)
1/2 cup bacon, diced
Fresh chives for garnish (optional)

Cooking Directions:

Begin by preparing the potato dough for the Halušky. Mix the grated potatoes with flour, egg, and a pinch of salt to form a thick, sticky dough. This dough is the foundation of the dish, bringing a comforting heartiness to every bite.

Bring a large pot of salted water to a boil. Using two spoons or a small ice cream scoop, form the potato dough into spaetzle-like dumplings and drop them into the boiling water. Cook them until they float to the surface, indicating they're cooked through. This process creates wonderfully textured dumplings — soft, yet with a satisfying bite.

While the dumplings are cooking, fry the diced bacon in a pan until it's crispy and golden. This crispy bacon not only adds a delightful crunch but also imparts a smoky richness to the dish.

In a separate bowl, prepare the bryndza cheese by mashing it to a spreadable consistency. If bryndza isn't available, a blend of feta and cream cheese can offer a similar tangy, creamy profile.

Once the Halušky are cooked, drain them and while still warm, mix them with the bryndza cheese. The heat from the dumplings will help the cheese melt slightly, creating a creamy coating for each piece.

Serve the Bryndzové Halušky topped with the crispy bacon bits. For an added touch of color and flavor, sprinkle some fresh chives on top.

And there you are! Lamb & Apricot Samosas. A bite that's a journey, from the bustling bazaars of Delhi to the fragrant souks of Marrakech. Paired with a minty dip or a cool raita, it's an experience not to be missed. Eat, savor, and let the stories flow.

Enjoy

17. Czech Bread Dumplings

Today, we're bringing a taste of the Czech Republic to your kitchen with Houskový Knedlík, or Czech Bread Dumplings. These dumplings are a unique blend of fluffy and dense textures, perfect for absorbing rich, savory sauces. In Czech cuisine, they are more than just a side dish; they are a symbol of comfort and a testament to the art of using simple ingredients to create something wonderfully satisfying. Let's embark on this culinary journey together.

Prep: 2 h. Cook: 20 min. Ready in: 2 h. 20 min. Servings: 4

Ingredients:

2 cups all-purpose flour

1/2 cup milk, lukewarm

2 teaspoons active dry yeast

1 tablespoon sugar

1/2 teaspoon salt

2 tablespoons butter, melted

1 egg

1 cup stale bread cubes

Cooking Directions:

Start by activating the yeast. In a small bowl, mix the lukewarm milk with sugar and yeast. Let it sit for about 10 minutes until it becomes frothy. This is where the magic begins, as the yeast comes to life.

In a large mixing bowl, combine the flour and salt. Make a well in the center and add the melted butter, egg, and the yeast mixture. Mix it together to form a soft, sticky dough. Now, gently fold in the stale bread cubes. These will give your dumplings a unique texture and a delightful flavor.

Knead the dough on a floured surface until it's smooth and elastic. Then, place it in a greased bowl, cover with a clean cloth, and let it rise in a warm place for about 1 hour, or until it doubles in size. This resting period allows the flavors to develop and the dough to become light and airy.

Once the dough has risen, divide it into two parts. Shape each part into a log, approximately the same length as your steamer or pot. Wrap each log loosely in a clean cloth, tying the ends with string.

Bring a large pot of water to a boil and carefully place the wrapped dumplings inside. Let them simmer for about 20 minutes, turning them halfway through the cooking time. The dumplings are done when they are puffed up and firm to the touch.

Carefully remove the dumplings from the pot and unwrap them. Let them cool slightly before slicing. Use a thread or a very sharp knife to cut the dumplings into slices. This method helps to preserve the soft texture without squishing them.

Serve the Houskový Knedlík alongside your favorite Czech meat dish, ready to soak up all the delicious flavors of the sauce.

And there you have it, Czech Bread Dumplings, a comforting and versatile addition to any hearty meal. This dish is a wonderful way to explore the rich and comforting flavors of Czech cuisine. Whether you're serving them with a savory stew or a saucy roast, these dumplings are sure to bring warmth and satisfaction to your dining table. Enjoy the process of making them, and as always, share the joy of homemade food with those around you. Dobrou chuť!

Enjoy

18. Russian Pelmini

Today, we're diving into the heart of Russian cooking with Pelmeni. These little dumplings are a culinary journey through Russian history, a dish that has warmed the hearts and bellies of families through the ages. Pelmeni are simple yet profoundly satisfying, encapsulating the robust and hearty nature of Russian cuisine. Let's embark on this delicious adventure together.

Prep: 60 min. Cook: 5 min. Ready in: 1 h. 5 min. Servings: 4

Ingredients:

For the Dough:

2 cups all-purpose flour
1/2 cup water
1 egg
1/2 teaspoon salt

For the Filling:

1/2 pound ground beef
1/2 pound ground pork
1 medium onion, finely chopped
Salt and pepper, to taste

For Serving:

Sour cream or melted butter
Fresh herbs like dill or parsley (optional)

Cooking Directions:

Start by making the dough. In a large bowl, mix together the flour, water, egg, and salt to form a smooth, elastic dough. Knead it on a floured surface until it's pliable and smooth. This dough needs to be tough enough to hold the filling but tender enough to melt in your mouth. Let it rest for about 30 minutes.

For the filling, combine the ground beef, ground pork, and finely chopped onion in a bowl. Season with salt and pepper. The filling should be flavorful and simple, allowing the taste of the meat to shine through.

Once the dough has rested, roll it out on a floured surface until it's thin. Use a small glass or cookie cutter to cut out circles.

Place a small amount of the meat filling in the center of each dough circle. Fold the dough over the filling to create a half-moon shape and pinch the edges to seal. Ensure they're well sealed to prevent the filling from escaping during cooking.

Bring a large pot of salted water to a boil. Carefully drop the Pelmeni into the water and cook them for about 5 minutes, or until they float to the surface. This is when they're perfectly cooked – the dough tender, and the filling juicy.

Serve the Pelmeni hot with a dollop of sour cream or a bit of melted butter. Garnish with fresh herbs like dill or parsley for an added touch of flavor and color.

And there you have it, traditional Russian Pelmeni, a dish that's as comforting as it is delicious. Whether it's a cold winter night or a gathering with friends and family, these dumplings are sure to be a hit. Enjoy the hearty flavors, the tender dough, and the joy of sharing a meal that's been cherished for generations. Приятного аппетита!

Enjoy

19. Swedish Kroppkaka

Today, we're bringing a piece of Swedish tradition to your kitchen with Kroppkaka. These dumplings are a beloved part of Swedish heritage, combining the earthy flavors of potato and pork with the warm, aromatic hint of allspice. Making Kroppkaka is more than just preparing a meal; it's an experience that connects you with the rustic charm and simplicity of Swedish countryside cooking. Let's roll up our sleeves and dive into this comforting and hearty dish.

Prep: 1 h. 30 min. Cook: 20 min. Ready in: 1 h. 50 min. Servings: 4

Ingredients:

For the Dough:

4 large potatoes, peeled

2-3 tablespoons all-purpose flour

1 egg

Salt, to taste'

For the Filling:

1/2 pound ground pork or bacon, finely chopped

1 large onion, finely chopped

1/2 teaspoon allspice

Salt and pepper, to taste

Cooking Directions:

Start by boiling the potatoes until they are tender. Once done, mash them thoroughly and let them cool slightly. This is your dough's base – a simple, humble potato transformed into something special.

In a large bowl, mix the mashed potatoes with flour, egg, and a bit of salt. You're aiming for a dough that is pliable but not too sticky. If it feels too wet, add a bit more flour. The texture is key – it should be firm enough to hold the filling but soft enough to yield a tender dumpling.

For the filling, sauté the chopped onion and pork or bacon until the onion is translucent and the meat is cooked through. Season this mixture with allspice, salt, and pepper. This filling should be aromatic and savory, with a subtle warmth from the allspice.

Now, it's time to assemble the Kroppkaka. Take a portion of the potato dough and flatten it in your hand. Place a spoonful of the meat filling in the center, then carefully wrap the dough around it, forming a ball. Make sure the filling is completely enclosed by the potato dough.

Bring a large pot of salted water to a boil. Carefully drop the dumplings into the water and let them cook for about 20 minutes. They are done when they float to the surface, a sign that the inside is cooked through and the outside is perfectly tender.

Serve the Kroppkaka warm, often accompanied by a dollop of butter or lingonberry jam. The contrast of the savory filling with the slightly sweet jam creates a delightful balance of flavors.

And there you have Swedish Kroppkaka, a dish that's as hearty as it is comforting. Whether enjoyed as part of a family dinner or a cozy meal on a chilly evening, these dumplings are sure to bring warmth and satisfaction to your table. Embrace the simple pleasures of Swedish cooking, and enjoy sharing these delicious dumplings with those you love. Smaklig måltid!

Enjoy

20. French Quenelles

We're taking a culinary voyage to France with the classic dish of Quenelles. This dish is the epitome of French sophistication and delicacy in cooking. Quenelles are about texture and finesse, combining simple yet high-quality ingredients to create something that's light yet rich in flavor. Let's immerse ourselves in the art of French cooking and prepare a dish that's sure to impress.

Prep: 60 min. Cook: 10 min. Ready in: 1 h. 10 min. Servings: 4

Ingredients:

For the Quenelles:

1/2 pound ground fish (like pike) or chicken

1/4 cup breadcrumbs

2 eggs

1/4 cup cream

Nutmeg, to taste

Salt and white pepper, to taste

For Poaching:

4 cups fish or chicken stock

For the Sauce (optional):

1 cup béchamel or Nantua sauce

Cooking Directions:

Begin by preparing the quenelle mixture. In a food processor, blend the ground fish or chicken until smooth. Add the breadcrumbs, eggs, cream, a pinch of nutmeg, salt, and white pepper. Blend until the mixture is homogeneous and smooth. It should be light and airy but hold its shape – the key to a perfect quenelle.

Let the mixture rest in the refrigerator for about 30 minutes. This resting time allows the flavors to meld and the texture to firm up slightly, making it easier to shape the quenelles.

Bring the fish or chicken stock to a gentle simmer in a wide, shallow pan. While it's heating, shape the quenelle mixture into oval dumplings using two spoons – one to scoop and the other to shape and smooth. This traditional technique might take a bit of practice, but it's a beautiful skill to master.

Gently lower the quenelles into the simmering stock. They should be poached gently to maintain their delicate texture. Cook them for about 10 minutes, or until they are firm and have risen to the surface.

If you're serving the quenelles with a sauce, prepare your béchamel or Nantua sauce. These classic French sauces add a luxurious richness to the light and delicate quenelles.

Serve the quenelles hot, bathed in your sauce of choice. Each bite should be a harmonious blend of the tender quenelle and the rich, creamy sauce – a true celebration of French culinary elegance.

Voilà, French Quenelles, a dish that's as refined as it is delightful. This recipe offers a glimpse into the sophistication of French cooking, where technique and quality ingredients come together to create something extraordinary. Enjoy these quenelles as a testament to your culinary skills, and share the elegance of French cuisine with friends and family. Bon appétit!

Enjoy

21. Southern Chicken and Dumplings

Today, we're embracing the heart and soul of Southern cooking with Chicken and Dumplings. This dish is more than just a meal; it's a comforting hug, a symbol of home and warmth. The combination of tender, flavorful chicken and soft, fluffy dumplings makes for a deeply satisfying experience. It's a culinary journey to the Southern states, where food is made with love and meant to be shared. Let's get started on this comforting classic.

Prep: 60 min. Cook: 30 min. Ready in: 1 h. 30 min. Servings: 4

Ingredients:

For the Chicken:

4 chicken thighs or breasts, bone-in and skin-on
6 cups chicken broth
1 onion, chopped
2 carrots, chopped
2 celery stalks, chopped
2 garlic cloves, minced
Salt and pepper, to taste
2 bay leaves
1 teaspoon dried thyme

For the Dumplings:

2 cups all-purpose flour
1 tablespoon baking powder
1/2 teaspoon salt
3 tablespoons unsalted butter, melted
3/4 cup milk

Cooking Directions:

Begin by cooking the chicken. In a large pot, combine the chicken, chicken broth, onion, carrots, celery, garlic, salt, pepper, bay leaves, and thyme. Bring it to a boil, then reduce the heat and simmer until the chicken is cooked through and tender. This creates a flavorful base for your dish, with the broth taking on the essence of the chicken and vegetables.

Once the chicken is cooked, remove it from the pot and let it cool. Then, shred the meat, discarding the skin and bones. Return the shredded chicken to the pot. The chicken should be tender and infused with the flavors of the broth and herbs.

For the dumplings, in a bowl, mix together flour, baking powder, and salt. Stir in the melted butter and milk to form a soft dough. It should be pliable and just a bit sticky.

Bring the broth to a gentle boil. Drop spoonfuls of the dumpling dough into the simmering broth. The dumplings will expand as they cook, so be sure not to overcrowd the pot. Cover and simmer for about 15 minutes, or until the dumplings are cooked through and fluffy. They should be like little clouds floating in the rich, savory broth.

Serve the Chicken and Dumplings hot. Each spoonful should bring together the tender chicken, the soft, pillowy dumplings, and the rich, flavorful broth.

And there you have it, Southern Chicken and Dumplings, a dish that's sure to warm your heart and fill your stomach. It's a taste of Southern hospitality, perfect for sharing with family and friends. Enjoy the comfort and joy that comes with each bite, and remember, the best meals are those made with love. Happy cooking!

Enjoy

22. Apple Dumplings

Embark on a delightful dessert adventure with Apple Dumplings, a beloved North American creation. Imagine the aroma of baked apples, cinnamon, and pastry filling your kitchen, creating an atmosphere of warmth and sweetness. Apple Dumplings are the perfect combination of tender, spiced apples wrapped in a flaky, buttery crust. Let's indulge in this delicious dessert that's sure to bring smiles and satisfaction.

Prep: 45 min. Cook: 40 min. Ready in: 1 h. 25 min. Servings: 4

Ingredients:

For the Dough:

2 cups all-purpose flour
1/2 teaspoon salt
2/3 cup unsalted butter, chilled and cut into pieces
4-6 tablespoons ice water

For the Filling:

4 medium-sized apples, peeled and cored
1/2 cup brown sugar
1 teaspoon cinnamon
1/4 teaspoon nutmeg
1/4 cup chopped pecans or walnuts (optional)
2 tablespoons unsalted butter, cut into small pieces

For Serving:

Vanilla ice cream or whipped cream (optional)
Caramel sauce (optional)

Cooking Directions:

Begin by making the dough. In a large bowl, combine the flour and salt. Add the chilled butter pieces and use a pastry cutter or your fingers to blend the butter into the flour until the mixture resembles coarse crumbs. Gradually add ice water, stirring until the dough comes together. Be careful not to overwork the dough; it should just hold together. Wrap the dough in plastic wrap and chill in the refrigerator for about 30 minutes. For the apple filling, mix the brown sugar, cinnamon, and nutmeg in a small bowl. If you're using nuts, stir them into the sugar mixture. This filling will infuse the apples with a lovely, warm spice flavor. Preheat your oven to 375°F (190°C). On a lightly floured surface, roll out the dough to about 1/8-inch thickness. Cut the dough into squares large enough to wrap around the apples.

Place an apple on each dough square. Fill the center of each apple with the sugar mixture and dot with a piece of butter. Carefully wrap the dough around each apple, sealing at the top. It's like tucking the apples into little pastry blankets.

Place the wrapped apples in a baking dish, ensuring they don't touch each other. If you like, you can brush the dough with a little milk or beaten egg for a golden finish.

Bake the dumplings for about 40 minutes, or until the crust is golden and the apples are tender. The aroma of baking apples and spices will be irresistible!

Serve the Apple Dumplings warm, perhaps with a scoop of vanilla ice cream, a dollop of whipped cream, or a drizzle of caramel sauce. Each bite combines the soft, spiced apple with the flaky crust, creating a dessert that's both comforting and delightful.

And there you have it, a sweet ending (or beginning) to any meal with these scrumptious Apple Dumplings. They're a testament to the simple joys of baking and the timeless appeal of apple desserts. Whether for a special occasion or a cozy night in, these dumplings are sure to be a hit. Enjoy the process, relish each bite, and as always, happy baking!

Enjoy

23. Drop Biscuit Dumplings

Today, we're bringing a touch of homestyle comfort to your table with Drop Biscuit Dumplings. These dumplings are a beloved addition to many American soups and stews, bringing a soft, bread-like texture that soaks up flavors beautifully. They are incredibly simple to make, yet they add a wonderful dimension to any dish they accompany. Let's whip up these fluffy, buttery dumplings and transform your next meal into a comforting feast.

Prep: 15 min. Cook: 15 min. Ready in: 30 min. Servings: 4

Ingredients:

2 cups all-purpose flour

1 tablespoon baking powder

1/2 teaspoon salt

1/2 teaspoon baking soda

4 tablespoons unsalted butter, chilled and cut into small pieces

3/4 cup buttermilk or milk

Fresh herbs like parsley or thyme, finely chopped (optional)

Cooking Directions:

Start by combining the flour, baking powder, salt, and baking soda in a large bowl. This is your dry mix, the base of your dumplings.

Add the chilled, cut-up butter to the dry ingredients. Use a pastry cutter or your fingers to work the butter into the flour until the mixture resembles coarse crumbs. This process is key to creating flaky, tender dumplings.

Stir in the buttermilk or milk just until the dough comes together. If you're using herbs, fold them in now. The dough should be sticky and a bit lumpy – don't overmix it.

Bring your soup or stew to a gentle simmer. Using a spoon or a small ice cream scoop, drop spoonfuls of the dumpling dough directly into the simmering liquid. The dumplings will expand as they cook, so leave some space between them.

Cover the pot and let the dumplings cook for about 15 minutes. Resist the temptation to peek; keeping the lid on helps them steam and puff up.

After 15 minutes, check the dumplings. They should be puffed up and firm to the touch. If they're not quite done, cover and cook for a few more minutes.

Serve the dumplings warm, nestled in your favorite soup or stew. Each dumpling should be a little cloud of comfort, soaking up the rich flavors of the dish.

And just like that, you've added a heartwarming touch to your meal with Drop Biscuit Dumplings. These simple, fluffy dumplings can elevate a simple soup or stew into something truly special. They're a reminder that sometimes the simplest things bring the greatest comfort. Enjoy the warmth and satisfaction they bring to your table, and as always, happy cooking!

Enjoy

24. Matzoh Ball Soup Dumplings

Today, we're embracing the warm and nurturing essence of Jewish cooking with Matzoh Ball Soup Dumplings. This dish is a heartwarming combination of light, fluffy matzoh balls and a simple yet flavorful chicken broth. Matzoh ball soup is often associated with comfort and tradition, bringing a sense of home and family to those who enjoy it. Let's prepare a dish that's as nourishing for the soul as it is for the body.

Prep: 60 min. Cook: 30 min. Ready in: 1 h. 30 min. Servings: 4

Ingredients:

For the Matzoh Balls:

1 cup matzoh meal
4 large eggs
1/4 cup vegetable oil or schmaltz (chicken fat)
1/4 cup chicken broth or water
1 teaspoon salt
A pinch of white pepper
2 tablespoons fresh parsley, finely chopped (optional)

For the Soup:

6 cups chicken broth
2 carrots, sliced
2 celery stalks, sliced
1 onion, quartered
Salt and pepper, to taste
Fresh dill, for garnish

Cooking Directions:

Begin by preparing the matzoh balls. In a bowl, beat the eggs with the oil or schmaltz. Add the matzoh meal, chicken broth or water, salt, white pepper, and parsley (if using). Mix everything until well combined. The mixture should be moist but firm enough to shape. Cover the bowl and refrigerate the matzoh ball mixture for at least 30 minutes. This chilling time helps the matzoh balls firm up and hold together during cooking.

While the matzoh ball mixture is chilling, prepare the soup. In a large pot, bring the chicken broth to a boil. Add the carrots, celery, and onion, and reduce the heat to a simmer. Season the broth with salt and pepper to taste. Let it simmer gently while the matzoh ball mixture chills.

After the matzoh ball mixture has chilled, wet your hands and form the mixture into balls, about the size of a walnut. The wet hands prevent the mixture from sticking and help create smoother balls.

Carefully drop the matzoh balls into the simmering broth. Cover the pot and let them cook for about 30 minutes. They're ready when they float to the surface and are tender all the way through.

Serve the matzoh ball soup hot, with a matzoh ball or two in each bowl, ladled with the broth and vegetables. Garnish with fresh dill for an added touch of flavor and freshness.

There you have Matzoh Ball Soup Dumplings, a dish that's rich in tradition and flavor. This soup is a celebration of simplicity and comfort, perfect for gatherings, holidays, or just a cozy night in. Each spoonful is a reminder of the power of food to comfort and connect us. Enjoy this timeless classic and the warmth it brings to your table.

Enjoy

25. Cornmeal Dumplings

Today we're embracing the rustic charm of Cornmeal Dumplings, a simple yet satisfying component that can transform a soup or stew into a hearty meal. These dumplings, with their grainy texture and mild flavor, are a testament to the humble cornmeal's versatility in cooking. Let's dive into this recipe, bringing a touch of comfort and simplicity to your kitchen.

Prep: 20 min. Cook: 20 min. Ready in: 40 min. Servings: 4

Ingredients:

1 cup cornmeal

1 cup all-purpose flour

1 teaspoon baking powder

1/2 teaspoon salt

3 tablespoons unsalted butter, melted

3/4 cup warm water or milk

Cooking Directions:

Start by mixing the cornmeal, flour, baking powder, and salt in a large bowl. This blend of dry ingredients forms the base of your dumplings, offering a nice balance between the coarseness of the cornmeal and the softness of the flour.

Pour in the melted butter and gradually add the warm water or milk. Stir the mixture until it comes together into a soft, cohesive dough. The dough should be moist but firm enough to hold its shape when formed. If it's too dry, add a little more water or milk; if it's too sticky, add a bit more flour.

Bring a pot of soup or stew to a gentle simmer. While it's heating, take small amounts of the dough and roll them into balls or small logs, depending on your preference. This is where you can get a little creative with the shapes.

Gently drop the dumplings into the simmering liquid. They will initially sink but should float to the surface as they cook and expand. Let them simmer for about 15-20 minutes. They're done when they have a firm texture and are cooked through.

Serve the cornmeal dumplings in a bowl of your favorite soup or stew. They should absorb some of the flavors of the liquid while maintaining a slight bite, adding both substance and depth to your meal.

And there you have it, Cornmeal Dumplings, a delightful addition to any soup or stew. This dish is a wonderful example of how simple ingredients can elevate a meal, adding both texture and heartiness. Enjoy these dumplings on a chilly day, or whenever you're in the mood for something comforting and satisfying. They're a reminder that sometimes, the simplest dishes can be the most rewarding.

Enjoy

26. Brazilian Coxinha

Today, we're diving into the vibrant world of Brazilian street food with Coxinha. This popular snack is loved throughout Brazil for its crispy exterior and rich, savory filling. Coxinha is more than just a treat; it's a cultural icon, a symbol of casual gatherings and festive occasions. Let's bring a taste of Brazil's lively streets to your kitchen with this delightful recipe.

Prep: 60 min. Cook: 30 min. Ready in: 1 h. 30 min. Servings: 4

Ingredients:

For the Filling:

2 tablespoons vegetable oil
1 small onion, finely chopped
2 cloves of garlic, minced
2 cups cooked chicken, shredded (seasoned with salt and pepper)
2 tablespoons tomato sauce
Salt and pepper, to taste
Chopped parsley and green onions, to taste

For the Dough:

2 cups chicken broth
2 tablespoons butter
2 cups all-purpose flour

For Coating and Frying:

2 eggs, beaten
2 cups breadcrumbs
Vegetable oil for frying

Cooking Directions:

Start by preparing the filling. Heat vegetable oil in a pan, sauté the onion and garlic until they're soft and fragrant. Add the shredded chicken, tomato sauce, salt, and pepper. Cook for a few minutes, then remove from heat and stir in chopped parsley and green onions. Set aside to cool. This filling should be moist and flavorful, embodying the heart of the coxinha.

For the dough, bring the chicken broth and butter to a boil in a large pot. Reduce the heat, add the flour all at once, and stir vigorously. Keep stirring until the dough comes together and pulls away from the sides of the pot. Turn off the heat and let it cool enough to handle.

To assemble the coxinhas, take a portion of the dough and flatten it in your hand. Place a spoonful of the chicken filling in the center, then mold the dough around the filling, shaping it into a teardrop or drumstick shape. This is where coxinha gets its characteristic look – each one should resemble a miniature chicken drumstick.

Once all the coxinhas are formed, dip them first in the beaten eggs and then roll them in breadcrumbs to coat. This coating is key to achieving that deliciously crispy exterior.

Heat vegetable oil in a deep fryer or a large deep pan to 350°F (175°C). Fry the coxinhas in batches until they are golden brown and crispy. Be sure not to overcrowd the pan to keep the oil temperature steady.

Serve the coxinhas warm, ideally with a tangy dipping sauce like Brazilian malagueta pepper sauce or a simple lime wedge. They should be crispy on the outside with a flavorful, juicy filling – a true taste of Brazilian cuisine.

And there you have it, Brazilian Coxinha, a snack that's as fun to make as it is to eat. These little drumsticks are a favorite at parties, gatherings, or just as a treat to enjoy any time. Dive into the flavors of Brazil and share these delicious bites with friends and family. Coxinha is not just food; it's an experience, a journey to the lively streets of Brazil. Bom apetite!

Enjoy

27. Argentine Empanadas

Today, we're bringing a piece of Argentina to your kitchen with their iconic Empanadas. These savory pastries are a celebration of flavors and textures, a beloved snack or meal enjoyed throughout Argentina. Whether served at a family gathering, a festive celebration, or enjoyed as a simple snack, empanadas are always a hit. Let's dive into this recipe and create a dish that's as enjoyable to prepare as it is to eat.

Prep: 60 min. Cook: 25 min. Ready in: 1 h. 25 min. Servings: 4

Ingredients:

For the Dough:

3 cups all-purpose flour
1/2 cup unsalted butter, chilled and cut into pieces
1 egg
1/2 cup water
1 teaspoon salt

For the Filling:

1 tablespoon olive oil
1 pound ground beef
1 large onion, finely chopped
2 cloves garlic, minced
1 teaspoon ground cumin
1/2 teaspoon paprika
1/4 cup green olives, chopped
1/4 cup raisins (optional)
Salt and pepper, to taste
2 hard-boiled eggs, chopped

Cooking Directions:

Begin by making the dough. In a large bowl, combine the flour and salt. Add the chilled butter and use a pastry cutter or your fingers to incorporate it into the flour until the mixture resembles coarse crumbs. Beat the egg with water and gradually add it to the flour mixture, mixing until a dough forms. Knead the dough briefly on a floured surface, then wrap it in plastic and let it rest in the refrigerator for about 30 minutes. For the filling, heat the olive oil in a pan over medium heat. Cook the ground beef and onion until the beef is browned and the onion is soft. Add the garlic, cumin, and paprika, cooking for a few more minutes. Stir in the green olives, raisins (if using), and season with salt and pepper. Remove from heat and let it cool, then mix in the chopped hard-boiled eggs. This filling should be rich, savory, and slightly tangy. Preheat your oven to 375°F (190°C) if you're baking the empanadas. On a floured surface, roll out the dough and cut it into circles. Spoon a portion of the beef filling onto each circle.

Fold the dough over the filling to create a half-moon shape. Seal the edges by pressing with a fork or twisting them decoratively. This sealing is crucial to prevent the filling from spilling out during cooking.

If baking, place the empanadas on a baking sheet lined with parchment paper and bake for about 25 minutes, or until they are golden brown. For frying, heat oil in a deep fryer or large skillet and fry the empanadas until they are golden and crispy.

Serve the empanadas warm, perhaps with a chimichurri sauce or a simple salsa for dipping. Each bite should offer a burst of the flavorful filling encased in a flaky, buttery crust – a true taste of Argentina.

And there you have Argentine Empanadas, a dish that's as versatile as it is delicious. These empanadas are perfect for any occasion – from a casual snack to a celebratory feast. Enjoy the process of making them, the joy of sharing them, and of course, the pleasure of eating them. Buen provecho!

Enjoy

28. Colombian Arepas.

Today, we're embracing the vibrant culture of Colombia with their beloved Arepas. These cornmeal cakes are a staple in Colombian households, enjoyed for their simplicity and versatility. Arepas can be enjoyed plain, stuffed, or topped with a variety of fillings, making them perfect for any meal of the day. Let's dive into this recipe and bring a taste of Colombia to your table.

Prep: 30 min. Cook: 15 min. Ready in: 45 min. Servings: 4

Ingredients:

2 cups pre-cooked white cornmeal (Masarepa)

2 1/2 cups warm water

1 teaspoon salt

1 tablespoon vegetable oil (plus more for cooking)

Optional fillings: shredded cheese, cooked meats, avocado, or beans

Cooking Directions:

Start by mixing the cornmeal, salt, and 1 tablespoon of vegetable oil in a large bowl. Gradually add the warm water, stirring continuously, until a soft dough forms. The dough should be pliable and not sticky. If it's too dry, add a little more water; if too wet, add a bit more cornmeal.

Let the dough rest for about 5 minutes. This resting time allows the cornmeal to fully hydrate and makes the dough easier to handle.

Divide the dough into equal portions and shape each one into a ball. Then, flatten each ball between your palms to form a cake about 1/2 inch thick. The arepas should be even in thickness to cook properly.

Heat a little vegetable oil in a large skillet over medium heat. Place the arepas in the skillet and cook for about 6-8 minutes on each side, or until they are golden brown and have a nice crust on both sides. The arepas should be crispy on the outside and soft on the inside.

Once cooked, you can split the arepas open and stuff them with your choice of fillings, like cheese, cooked meats, avocado, or beans. Alternatively, you can serve them whole and top them with your favorite toppings.

Serve the arepas warm, as a side dish, a main course, or even as a snack. They are a canvas for a variety of flavors and are always a comforting and satisfying option.

And there you have Colombian Arepas, a simple yet delightful dish that's a cornerstone of Colombian cuisine. Whether you enjoy them stuffed, topped, or plain, arepas are a wonderful way to explore the flavors of Colombia. Share them with family and friends, and enjoy the versatility and comfort they bring to your table. ¡Buen provecho!

Enjoy

29. Bolivian Salteñas

Today, we're bringing the flavors of Bolivia to your kitchen with Salteñas. These pastries are a culinary icon in Bolivian cuisine, known for their unique, slightly sweet crust and rich, savory filling. Making Salteñas is a delightful experience, combining the art of pastry with the robust flavors of Bolivian cooking. Let's embark on this culinary adventure and create a dish that's bursting with flavor and tradition.

Prep: 120 min. Cook: 45 min. Ready in: 2 h. 45 min. Servings: 4

Ingredients:

For the Dough:

3 cups all-purpose flour
1/2 cup sugar
1/2 teaspoon salt
1/2 cup unsalted butter, chilled and cut into pieces
2 eggs
1/2 cup water (more if needed)

For the Filling:

1 tablespoon vegetable oil
1 pound ground beef or chicken
1 large onion, finely chopped
1 green bell pepper, finely chopped
2 cloves garlic, minced
1 teaspoon cumin
1 teaspoon paprika
1/2 cup beef or chicken broth
1/2 cup peas
1/2 cup diced potatoes
1/4 cup chopped olives
2 hard-boiled eggs, chopped
Salt and pepper, to taste

For Glaze:

1 egg yolk, beaten with a tablespoon of water

Cooking Directions:

Start by making the dough. In a large bowl, combine the flour, sugar, and salt. Add the chilled butter, cutting it into the flour until the mixture resembles coarse crumbs. Beat the eggs and mix them with water, then gradually add to the flour mixture. Knead until a smooth dough forms, adding more water if necessary. The dough should be pliable but not sticky. Wrap it in plastic and let it rest in the refrigerator for about 1 hour.

For the filling, heat oil in a large skillet over medium heat. Cook the ground beef or chicken until browned. Add the onion, green bell pepper, and garlic, sautéing until the vegetables are soft. Stir in cumin, paprika, broth, peas, potatoes, and olives. Cook until the potatoes are tender. Season with salt and pepper, then let the mixture cool. Once cooled, mix in the chopped hard-boiled eggs.

Preheat your oven to 375°F (190°C).

Roll out the dough on a floured surface and cut it into circles. Spoon a portion of the filling onto each circle, then fold the dough over to create a crescent shape. Seal the edges by crimping, ensuring the filling is completely enclosed.

Brush the Salteñas with the egg yolk and water mixture for a golden finish.

Place the Salteñas on a baking sheet lined with parchment paper and bake for about 30 to 45 minutes, or until they are golden brown.

Serve the Salteñas warm, allowing the rich and savory flavors to shine through. These pastries are not just a meal; they're an experience, a taste of Bolivia's culinary heritage.

And there you have it, Bolivian Salteñas, a dish that's as vibrant and flavorful as the country it comes from. Whether you're exploring new cuisines or revisiting familiar flavors, Salteñas are sure to delight and satisfy. Enjoy these savory pastries with friends and family, and take pride in the culinary journey you've embarked on. ¡Buen provecho!

Enjoy

30. Moroccan Chicken Pastilla

Today we're venturing into the aromatic and vibrant world of Moroccan cuisine with Chicken Pastilla. This dish is a splendid fusion of flavors and textures, combining sweet, savory, and spicy elements in a flaky, golden pastry. Pastilla is a celebration, often served at special occasions, embodying the complexity and richness of Moroccan cooking. Let's create this culinary masterpiece and take your taste buds on an unforgettable journey.

Prep: 1 h. 30 min. Cook: 45 min. Ready in: 2 h. 15 min. Servings: 4

Ingredients:

For the Filling:

2 tablespoons olive oil
4 chicken thighs, bone-in and skin-on
1 large onion, finely chopped
2 cloves garlic, minced
1 teaspoon ground cinnamon
1/2 teaspoon ground ginger
1/2 teaspoon ground turmeric
1/4 teaspoon saffron threads
2 cups chicken broth
4 eggs, beaten
1/2 cup chopped fresh cilantro
1/2 cup chopped fresh parsley
Salt and pepper, to taste
1 cup almonds, toasted and roughly chopped

For Assembly:

8-10 sheets phyllo dough, thawed
1/2 cup unsalted butter, melted
Powdered sugar and ground cinnamon, for dusting

Cooking Directions:

Begin by heating olive oil in a large skillet. Add the chicken thighs and cook until browned on both sides. Add the onion and garlic, sautéing until soft. Stir in the cinnamon, ginger, turmeric, and saffron, coating the chicken and onions with the spices. Pour in the chicken broth, bring to a simmer, cover, and cook until the chicken is tender.

Remove the chicken from the broth and let it cool. Then, shred the meat, discarding the skin and bones. Return the shredded chicken to the skillet.

Preheat your oven to 375°F (190°C).

In the same skillet with the chicken, add the beaten eggs, cilantro, and parsley. Cook, stirring, until the eggs are set. Season the mixture with salt and pepper, then stir in the chopped almonds. This is your pastilla filling, a rich and fragrant blend of sweet and savory.

To assemble the pastilla, brush a sheet of phyllo dough with melted butter and lay another sheet on top. Repeat this process until you have a stack of 4-5 sheets. Place some of the filling in the center, then fold the phyllo over the filling to create a parcel. Repeat with the remaining phyllo and filling.

Place the pastilla parcels on a baking sheet, brush the tops with more melted butter, and bake for about 25-30 minutes, or until golden and crisp.

Dust the baked pastilla with powdered sugar and a sprinkle of ground cinnamon just before serving.

And there you have Moroccan Chicken Pastilla, a dish that's as visually stunning as it is delicious. Each bite offers a delightful contrast of flavors and textures, from the crispy phyllo to the rich, spiced filling. Pastilla is a celebration of Moroccan culture and cuisine, perfect for special occasions or whenever you want to create something truly extraordinary. Enjoy this beautiful blend of sweet and savory and let the flavors of Morocco transport you to a world of culinary wonders. Bon appétit!

Enjoy

31. South African Steak Bunny Chow

Today, we're diving into the vibrant world of South African cuisine with Steak Bunny Chow. This dish is a hearty, flavorful, and unique meal that has become a symbol of South African street food culture. It combines the rich, spicy flavors of Indian curry with a quintessentially South African twist. Let's create this comforting and satisfying dish that's perfect for sharing and sure to be a conversation starter.

Prep: 60 min. Cook: 2 h. Ready in: 3 h. Servings: 4

Ingredients:

For the Steak Curry:

2 pounds beef steak, cut into cubes

2 tablespoons vegetable oil

1 large onion, finely chopped

3 cloves garlic, minced

1 tablespoon ginger, grated

2 tablespoons curry powder

1 teaspoon ground cumin

1 teaspoon ground coriander

1/2 teaspoon turmeric

1 can (14 oz) diced tomatoes

1 can (14 oz) coconut milk

Salt and pepper, to taste

2-3 potatoes, peeled and cubed

Fresh cilantro, for garnish

For the Bunny Chow:

1 large loaf white bread, unsliced

Cooking Directions:

Begin by preparing the steak curry. Heat the vegetable oil in a large pot over medium heat. Add the steak cubes and brown them on all sides. Remove the steak and set it aside.

In the same pot, add the onion, garlic, and ginger, sautéing until the onion is soft and translucent. Stir in the curry powder, cumin, coriander, and turmeric, cooking for a minute until the spices are fragrant.

Add the diced tomatoes, coconut milk, and browned steak back into the pot. Season with salt and pepper. Bring the mixture to a boil, then reduce the heat and let it simmer for about 1.5 to 2 hours, or until the steak is tender and the sauce has thickened. About 30 minutes before the curry is done, add the cubed potatoes and continue to simmer.

While the curry is cooking, prepare the bread. Cut the loaf of bread in half and hollow out the center of each half, leaving a thick wall and base. This will be your "bowl" for the curry.

Once the curry is ready and the potatoes are cooked, spoon the hot steak curry into the hollowed-out bread loaves. Garnish with fresh cilantro.

And there you have it, South African Steak Bunny Chow, a dish bursting with flavors and textures. It's a fun and communal dish, perfect for sharing with friends and family. Enjoy the hearty curry soaked up by the soft bread, and dive into the rich history and cultural fusion that this dish represents. It's a true taste of South Africa's diverse and vibrant culinary landscape.

Enjoy

32. Nigerian Moi Moi (Bean Dumplings)

Today, we're exploring the rich and diverse flavors of Nigerian cuisine with Moi Moi, a beloved and nutritious bean pudding. Moi Moi is revered for its smooth texture and flavorful blend of beans and spices. This dish is a staple in Nigerian households, often served at gatherings and celebrations. Let's delve into this recipe and bring a taste of Nigeria to your kitchen.

Prep: 60 min. Cook: 60 min. Ready in: 2 h. Servings: 4

Ingredients:

2 cups black-eyed peas, soaked overnight and skins removed

1 medium onion, chopped

1 red bell pepper, chopped

1 scotch bonnet pepper (adjust to taste), chopped

2 cloves garlic, minced

1/2 cup vegetable oil

2 tablespoons ground crayfish (optional)

2-3 tablespoons tomato paste

2 eggs, hard-boiled and sliced (optional)

Salt and seasoning cubes (Maggi or Knorr), to taste

Banana leaves or aluminum foil, for wrapping

Cooking Directions:

Begin by preparing the beans. Soak the black-eyed peas overnight, then remove the skins the next day. This can be done by rubbing the beans between your hands or in a blender with water, then draining off the skins. Blend the soaked and skinned black-eyed peas with onion, red bell pepper, scotch bonnet pepper, and garlic until smooth. You're aiming for a thick but pourable batter.

Transfer the bean mixture to a bowl. Stir in the vegetable oil, ground crayfish (if using), tomato paste, salt, and seasoning cubes. Mix thoroughly to ensure the spices and oil are well distributed.

If using eggs, slice the hard-boiled eggs and set them aside. You can also add other ingredients like cooked fish or corned beef to the mixture for variety.

Prepare your steaming apparatus - either banana leaves or aluminum foil. If using banana leaves, briefly pass them over an open flame to make them more pliable. Cut them into sheets large enough to hold a scoop of the bean mixture.

Scoop some of the bean mixture onto the center of each banana leaf or aluminum foil sheet. If you're adding egg slices or other fillings, place them on top of the mixture before sealing.

Fold the leaves or foil around the mixture to form a secure package. Ensure they're well-sealed so the Moi Moi can steam properly.

Steam the Moi Moi for about 1 hour. You can do this in a steamer or by placing them in a pot over a rack and adding water to the bottom of the pot. The Moi Moi is done when it solidifies and is firm to the touch.

Serve the Moi Moi warm as a side dish or as part of a larger meal. It's often enjoyed with rice, stews, or as a standalone snack.

And there you have Nigerian Moi Moi, a dish that's as nourishing as it is flavorful. This recipe is a celebration of Nigerian culinary traditions, showcasing the versatility of simple ingredients like beans and spices. Enjoy the unique texture and rich taste of Moi Moi, and share this delightful dish with friends and family. Bon appétit!

Enjoy

33. Kenyan Ugali

Today, we're embracing the essence of Kenyan cooking with Ugali, a beloved and fundamental part of Kenyan and East African cuisine. This dish is valued for its simplicity and ability to complement a variety of main courses. Ugali is about the joy of sharing a meal, a communal dish often enjoyed with friends and family. Let's dive into this quintessential Kenyan staple.

Prep: 10 min. Cook: 20 min. Ready in: 30 min. Servings: 4

Ingredients:

4 cups water

2 cups white cornmeal (finely ground)

Salt (optional)

Cooking Directions:

Start by bringing the water to a boil in a large pot. If you prefer, add a pinch of salt to the water.

Gradually whisk in the white cornmeal. Reduce the heat to a medium-low and continue to stir. The key to great ugali is in the stirring; you want to prevent lumps from forming and ensure an even consistency.

Continue to cook the mixture, stirring constantly. As it thickens, switch from a whisk to a wooden spoon. The ugali will become quite thick and start to pull away from the sides of the pot. This process usually takes about 15 to 20 minutes.

Once the ugali has reached a firm, dough-like consistency, remove it from the heat. Let it cool for a few moments, just enough to handle.

To serve, wet your hands slightly with water and shape the ugali into a round, smooth mound. Place it on a serving plate or dish. Ugali is traditionally eaten with your hands – pinch off a piece, roll it into a ball, and make an indentation to scoop up accompanying stews or dishes.

Serve the ugali warm alongside your favorite vegetable dish, stew, or any other dish with a sauce or gravy. It's a versatile side that complements a wide range of flavors.

And there you have it, Kenyan Ugali, a dish that's as much about the experience as it is about taste. This simple yet satisfying staple is a testament to the beauty of African cuisine, where food is about community, sharing, and simplicity. Enjoy the heartwarming simplicity of Ugali, a perfect canvas for a variety of flavorful dishes.

Enjoy

34. Potato & Pea Dumplings

Today we're making Potato & Pea Dumplings, a beloved snack and appetizer across the Indian subcontinent and beyond. These delightful dumplings, with their crispy outer shell and flavorful filling, are a fusion of textures and tastes. Making dumplings is a joyful process, from preparing the spiced filling to shaping the perfect pastry. Let's bring the magic of Indian street food to your kitchen with this recipe.

Prep: 60 min. Cook: 30 min. Ready in: 1 h. 30 min. Servings: 4

Ingredients:

For the Dough:

2 cups all-purpose flour
1/4 cup vegetable oil
1/2 teaspoon salt
Approximately 1/2 cup water

For the Filling:

2 large potatoes, boiled, peeled, and mashed
1 cup green peas, boiled
1 tablespoon vegetable oil
1 teaspoon cumin seeds
1 small onion, finely chopped
1 teaspoon grated ginger
1 teaspoon grated garlic
1 teaspoon ground coriander
1 teaspoon garam masala
1/2 teaspoon red chili powder
Salt to taste
Fresh cilantro, chopped
Vegetable oil for frying

Cooking Directions:

Begin with the dough. In a large bowl, mix the flour, salt, and oil. Gradually add water and knead to form a firm dough. It should be smooth and pliable, not too soft. Cover the dough and let it rest while you prepare the filling.

For the filling, heat a tablespoon of oil in a pan. Add the cumin seeds and let them sputter. Then add the onions, ginger, and garlic, sautéing until the onions are translucent.

Add the mashed potatoes and peas to the pan. Stir in the ground coriander, garam masala, red chili powder, and salt. Cook for a few minutes until the mixture is well combined and fragrant. Remove from heat and add chopped cilantro. Allow the filling to cool.

Divide the dough into equal-sized balls. Roll out each ball into a thin oval shape, then cut it in half to form two semi-circles.

Take one semi-circle, apply water along the edge, and form it into a cone shape by pinching the straight edge together. Fill the cone with the potato and pea mixture, then seal the open edges, forming the shape.

Heat oil in a deep pan. Fry the dumplings in batches until they are golden brown and crispy. Be sure to fry them over medium heat to ensure they cook evenly.

Serve the dumplings hot with chutneys or ketchup, perfect as a snack or appetizer. Each bite offers a crunchy exterior with a deliciously spiced interior, making them irresistible.

And there you have it, Potato & Pea Dumplings, a classic dish that brings the flavors of the Indian subcontinent to your table. Enjoy these samosas with friends and family, and delight in the blend of spices, textures, and tastes. Whether you're an experienced cook or trying Indian cuisine for the first time, this dish is sure to be a hit.

Enjoy

35. Paneer Momo

Today, we're embracing the fusion of flavors with Paneer Momo, a dish that brings together the delicate art of dumpling making with the rich textures and flavors of Indian cuisine. These dumplings are a popular street food in South Asia, and the addition of paneer makes them exceptionally delicious and satisfying. Let's create these tender pockets of joy, filled with spiced paneer and vegetables.

Prep: 60 min. Cook: 10 min. Ready in: 1 h. 10 min. Servings: 4

Ingredients:

For the Dough:
2 cups all-purpose flour
1/2 teaspoon salt
About 3/4 cup water

For the Filling:
1 cup paneer, crumbled or finely chopped
1/2 cup cabbage, finely chopped
1/2 cup carrots, grated
1/2 cup onion, finely chopped
2 cloves garlic, minced
1 inch ginger, grated
1 green chili, finely chopped (optional)
1 tablespoon soy sauce
1 teaspoon sesame oil
Salt and pepper, to taste
Fresh cilantro, chopped

For Steaming:
Cabbage leaves or parchment paper

Cooking Directions:

Begin with the dough. In a large mixing bowl, combine the flour and salt. Gradually add water, kneading until you form a smooth and pliable dough. The dough should not be too sticky or too dry. Cover it and let it rest while you prepare the filling.

For the filling, in a mixing bowl, combine the crumbled paneer, cabbage, carrots, onion, garlic, ginger, and green chili. Add soy sauce, sesame oil, salt, pepper, and cilantro. Mix everything well, ensuring that the flavors are evenly distributed throughout the paneer and vegetables.

Once the dough has rested, divide it into small portions and roll each portion into a ball. Then, on a lightly floured surface, roll out each ball into a thin circle.

Place a small amount of the paneer filling in the center of each dough circle. Carefully bring the edges of the dough together and pinch to seal, creating a pleated pattern. Make sure the momos are sealed well to prevent the filling from leaking out during steaming.

Prepare your steamer by lining it with cabbage leaves or parchment paper. This prevents the momos from sticking to the bottom. Arrange the momos in the steamer, making sure they don't touch each other.

Steam the momos for about 10 minutes or until the dough becomes translucent and glossy. The steaming process cooks both the dough and filling, infusing the momos with a delicate flavor.

Serve the Paneer Momos hot, accompanied by a spicy dipping sauce like chutney or hot garlic sauce. Each bite should be a delightful mix of the soft, tender dough and the flavorful, juicy filling.

And there you have it, Paneer Momos, a dish that's both comforting and exotic. These dumplings are a perfect example of the culinary diversity found in the Indian subcontinent. Enjoy them as a snack, an appetizer, or a main course, and savor the delightful blend of textures and flavors.

Enjoy

36. Lentil Dumpling (Dahi Vada)

Today, we're diving into the flavorsome world of Indian cuisine with Dahi Vada. This dish is a beloved staple in Indian cooking, known for its harmonious blend of soft, spongy lentil dumplings, creamy yogurt, and vibrant chutneys. Dahi Vada is not only a treat for the palate but also a feast for the eyes, often served at festivals and celebrations. Let's create this delightful dish that's both refreshing and satisfying.

Prep: 60 min. Cook: 30 min. Ready in: 1 h. 30 min. Servings: 4

Ingredients:

For the Lentil Dumplings:

1 cup urad dal (split black lentils), soaked for 4-6 hours
Salt, to taste
Oil, for deep frying

For Serving:

2 cups plain yogurt, whisked
1/2 teaspoon roasted cumin powder
1/2 teaspoon red chili powder
1/2 teaspoon chaat masala
Tamarind chutney
Mint-coriander chutney
Salt, to taste
Fresh coriander (cilantro), for garnish

Cooking Directions:

Begin by preparing the lentil dumplings. Drain the soaked urad dal and grind it into a smooth paste, adding very little water. The batter should be thick and fluffy. Add salt to taste.

Heat oil in a deep frying pan over medium heat. Wet your hands and take a small amount of the dal batter, shape it into a ball, and gently slide it into the hot oil. Fry the vadas until they are golden brown and crispy. Drain them on paper towels.

Once all the vadas are fried, soak them in warm water for about 20 minutes. This step ensures they become soft and spongy. Gently press the vadas between your palms to remove excess water and arrange them in a serving dish.

Whisk the plain yogurt until smooth. Add a little water if it's too thick. Season the yogurt with salt, then pour it over the vadas, ensuring they are completely covered.

Sprinkle roasted cumin powder, red chili powder, and chaat masala over the yogurt. Drizzle tamarind chutney and mint-coriander chutney on top. These chutneys add a tangy, spicy, and sweet flavor to the dish. Garnish with fresh coriander leaves and serve the Dahi Vada chilled or at room temperature.

There you have Dahi Vada, a classic dish that beautifully encapsulates the essence of Indian cuisine. Each bite offers a burst of flavors - the tanginess of yogurt, the richness of the vadas, and the zing from the chutneys. This dish is perfect for hot summer days, as a snack, appetizer, or part of a larger meal. Enjoy the delightful interplay of tastes and textures in this much-loved Indian delicacy.

Enjoy

37. Malabar Chicken Paratha

Today, we're embracing the rich and diverse culinary traditions of the Indian subcontinent with Malabar Chicken Paratha. This dish is a delightful blend of tender, spiced chicken encased in a flaky, buttery flatbread. It's a popular street food in India, known for its irresistible layers and mouth-watering filling. Let's dive into this recipe and bring a taste of the Malabar coast to your kitchen.

Prep: 1 h. 30 min. Cook: 30 min. Ready in: 2 h. Servings: 4

Ingredients:

For the Paratha Dough:

3 cups all-purpose flour
1 teaspoon salt
2 tablespoons oil
Approximately 1 cup water

For the Chicken Filling:

2 tablespoons vegetable oil
1 pound boneless, skinless chicken breasts, finely chopped
1 large onion, finely chopped
2 cloves garlic, minced
1 inch ginger, minced
2 green chilies, finely chopped
1 teaspoon ground turmeric
1 teaspoon garam masala
1 teaspoon ground coriander
1/2 teaspoon red chili powder
2 tablespoons fresh cilantro, chopped
Salt to taste

Cooking Directions:

Begin with the paratha dough. In a large bowl, mix the flour and salt. Gradually add water and oil, kneading until a soft, elastic dough forms. The dough should be pliable but not sticky. Cover and let it rest for about 30 minutes.

For the chicken filling, heat oil in a pan over medium heat. Sauté the onions, garlic, ginger, and green chilies until the onions are translucent. Add the finely chopped chicken and cook until it's no longer pink.

Stir in the turmeric, garam masala, ground coriander, and red chili powder. Cook for a few more minutes until the chicken is fully cooked and the spices are well integrated. Season with salt and finish with chopped cilantro. Let the filling cool down.

Divide the rested dough into equal-sized balls. Roll out one ball into a thin circle. Spread a small amount of oil over the surface, then fold it into a semi-circle, and fold again into a quarter circle. Roll out this quarter circle into a thin layer once more.

Place a portion of the chicken filling in the center of the rolled-out dough. Fold the edges over the filling, sealing it completely.

Heat a skillet or griddle over medium heat. Place the filled paratha on the skillet and cook until both sides are golden brown and crispy, applying a little oil or butter to each side.

Serve the Malabar Chicken Paratha hot, ideally with a side of raita, pickle, or curry. Each bite should offer a burst of spiced chicken filling wrapped in a flaky, buttery bread.

There you have Malabar Chicken Paratha, a dish that's as enjoyable to make as it is to eat. This recipe is a beautiful way to explore the flavors of the Indian subcontinent, perfect for a special meal or a weekend treat. Enjoy the layers of flavor and texture in each bite, and share this delightful culinary experience with your loved ones.

Enjoy

38. Gujiya (Sweet Dumplings)

Today, we're delving into the sweet and aromatic world of Gujiya, a delightful confection that's deeply rooted in the culinary traditions of the Indian subcontinent. These sweet dumplings are a festival favorite, embodying the joy and celebration of special occasions. Gujiya's combination of creamy filling and crispy exterior makes it a delectable treat. Let's indulge in the art of making Gujiya and add a sweet note to your cooking repertoire.

Prep: 60 min. Cook: 30 min. Ready in: 1 h. 30 min. Servings: 4

Ingredients:

For the Dough:

2 cups all-purpose flour
1/4 cup ghee (clarified butter)
A pinch of salt
Water, as needed to form the dough

For the Filling:

1 cup khoya or mawa (dried whole milk)
1/2 cup powdered sugar
1/2 cup mixed nuts (almonds, cashews, pistachios), finely chopped
1/4 cup raisins
1/2 teaspoon cardamom powder
A pinch of nutmeg

For Frying:

Vegetable oil or ghee, for deep frying

Cooking Directions:

Start by making the dough. In a large mixing bowl, combine the flour, a pinch of salt, and ghee. Rub the ghee into the flour with your fingertips until it resembles breadcrumbs. Gradually add water and knead to form a stiff dough. The dough should be firm but pliable. Cover and let it rest for about 30 minutes.

For the filling, crumble the khoya or mawa in a pan over low heat until it's soft and warm. Remove from heat and let it cool. Add powdered sugar, chopped nuts, raisins, cardamom powder, and nutmeg to the khoya. Mix well. This sweet and nutty mixture is the heart of your Gujiya.

Divide the dough into small balls. Roll each ball into a small, thin circle. Place a spoonful of the filling on one half of the circle, leaving the edges clear.

Moisten the edges of the dough with a little water. Fold the dough over the filling to form a semi-circle. Seal the edges by pressing them together, then use a fork or a Gujiya mold to create a decorative edge.

Heat the oil or ghee in a deep frying pan over medium heat. Fry the Gujiya in batches, turning them occasionally, until they are golden and crisp.

Drain the Gujiya on paper towels and let them cool. They can be stored in an airtight container for several days.

Serve the Gujiya as a delightful dessert or a special treat. Each bite offers a crispy shell giving way to a rich, sweet, and spiced filling – a true celebration of flavors.

And there you have it, Gujiya, a classic sweet that captures the essence of festivity and celebration in the Indian subcontinent. Whether you're marking a special occasion or simply craving something sweet, these dumplings are sure to delight. Enjoy the process of making them and the joy of sharing these sweet treats with friends and family.

Enjoy

39. Turkish Manti (Lamb Dumplings)

Today, we're diving into the rich and aromatic world of Turkish cuisine with Manti. This dish is a celebrated part of Turkish culinary tradition, known for its delicate dumplings and flavorful accompaniments. The process of making Manti is almost as enjoyable as eating it, requiring a bit of patience and a lot of love. Let's create this exquisite dish, bringing a taste of Turkey to your home.

Prep: 60 min. Cook: 20 min. Ready in: 1 h. 20 min. Servings: 4

Ingredients:

For the Dough:

2 cups all-purpose flour
1 egg
1/2 cup water
1/2 teaspoon salt

For the Filling:

1/2 pound ground lamb
1 small onion, finely grated
1 clove garlic, minced
1 teaspoon ground cumin
1/2 teaspoon ground coriander
Salt and pepper, to taste

For Serving:

1 cup plain yogurt
2 tablespoons butter
1 teaspoon paprika
Dried mint, for garnish

Cooking Directions:

Begin with the dough. In a mixing bowl, combine the flour, egg, water, and salt. Knead until the dough is smooth and elastic. Let it rest for about 30 minutes, covered, to allow the gluten to relax.

For the filling, mix together the ground lamb, grated onion, minced garlic, cumin, coriander, salt, and pepper. The mixture should be well-seasoned and aromatic.

Once the dough has rested, roll it out on a lightly floured surface as thinly as possible. Cut the dough into small squares, about 2 inches each.

Place a small amount of the lamb filling in the center of each square. Fold the dough over to form a triangle, pinching the edges to seal. Then, bring the two opposite corners of the triangle together and pinch to form a small "bundle." This shape is characteristic of traditional Turkish Manti.

Bring a large pot of salted water to a boil. Add the Manti in batches, being careful not to overcrowd the pot. Cook them for about 10-15 minutes, or until they rise to the surface and are cooked through.

While the Manti are cooking, prepare the sauce. Melt the butter in a small pan, add the paprika, and remove from heat.

To serve, place the boiled Manti on a serving dish. Spoon over some plain yogurt and drizzle with the spicy butter sauce. Garnish with dried mint.

And there you have it, Turkish Manti, a dish that's as delightful to look at as it is to eat. Each dumpling is a small bundle of joy, bursting with flavors that are both rich and subtle. This dish is perfect for a special occasion or when you want to explore the depths of Turkish cuisine. Enjoy the blend of textures and flavors, and share this culinary delight with your loved ones. Afiyet olsun!

Enjoy

40. Kurdish Kubbeh

Today, we're exploring the rich and hearty flavors of Kurdish cuisine with Kubbeh. This dish is a cornerstone of Kurdish cooking, celebrated for its unique texture and depth of flavor. Kubbeh combines the nuttiness of bulgur with a savory, spiced meat filling, often enjoyed in a nourishing broth. Let's delve into the process of making this traditional dish, bringing the essence of Kurdish culture to your kitchen.

Prep: 1 h. 30 min. Cook: 30 min. Ready in: 2 h. Servings: 4

Ingredients:

For the Shell:

2 cups fine bulgur wheat

1/2 cup semolina

Water (as needed)

Salt (to taste)

For the Filling:

1 pound ground lamb or beef

1 medium onion, finely chopped

1 teaspoon ground allspice

1/2 teaspoon ground cinnamon

1/2 teaspoon ground cumin

Salt and pepper, to taste

1/4 cup pine nuts (optional)

For the Broth (optional):

6 cups beef or chicken broth

1 onion, quartered

2 carrots, chopped

2 celery stalks, chopped

Salt and pepper, to taste

Fresh herbs for garnish

Cooking Directions:

Begin with the shell. Soak the fine bulgur wheat in warm water for about 30 minutes until it's softened. Drain any excess water and mix in the semolina, adding a little water if necessary, to form a dough-like consistency. Season with salt. The mixture should be pliable and hold together well.

For the filling, heat a skillet over medium heat. Cook the ground lamb or beef with the onion until the meat is browned and the onion is soft. Drain any excess fat. Add the allspice, cinnamon, cumin, salt, and pepper, stirring well to combine. If using, add the pine nuts towards the end of cooking. Let the filling cool.

To form the kubbeh, take a small amount of the bulgur mixture and flatten it in your palm to form a thin layer. Place a spoonful of the meat filling in the center. Carefully enclose the filling with the bulgur mixture, forming an oval or ball shape. Repeat with the remaining bulgur and filling.

If making broth, combine the beef or chicken broth with the onion, carrots, and celery in a large pot. Bring to a boil, then reduce to a simmer. Season with salt and pepper.

Gently add the kubbeh to the simmering broth and cook for about 20-30 minutes, or until they are cooked through, and the bulgur is tender. Serve the kubbeh in the broth, garnished with fresh herbs. Alternatively, they can be served dry, alongside yogurt or a salad.

There you have Kurdish Kubbeh, a dish that's as nourishing as it is flavorful. This traditional recipe offers a glimpse into the soul of Kurdish cuisine, where every bite tells a story of heritage and culinary art. Enjoy these delicious dumplings with family and friends, and savor the rich, comforting flavors they bring to your table. Şerefe!

Enjoy

41. Persian Gondhi (Chicken Chickpea Dumplings)

Today, we're delving into the flavors of Persian cuisine with Gondhi, a unique and delightful dish. These chicken and chickpea dumplings are a testament to the rich and aromatic flavors of Persian cooking. Gondhi is often served in a clear broth, making it a comforting and hearty meal. Let's embark on this culinary journey and bring a taste of Persia to your table.

Prep: 60 min. Cook: 30 min. Ready in: 1 h. 30 min. Servings: 4

Ingredients:

For the Gondhi:

1 pound ground chicken
1 cup chickpea flour
1 large onion, grated
1 teaspoon turmeric
1/2 teaspoon ground cardamom
Salt and pepper, to taste
2 tablespoons vegetable oil

For the Broth:

6 cups chicken broth
1 onion, quartered
2 carrots, chopped
2 celery stalks, chopped
A few sprigs of fresh parsley
Salt and pepper, to taste
Lemon juice (optional)

Cooking Directions:

Begin by preparing the gondhi mixture. In a large bowl, combine the ground chicken, chickpea flour, grated onion, turmeric, cardamom, salt, and pepper. Mix well until all the ingredients are thoroughly combined. The mixture should be firm enough to form into balls.

Form the chicken mixture into medium-sized balls, about the size of a golf ball. Coat your hands with vegetable oil to prevent sticking.

Prepare the broth. In a large pot, bring the chicken broth to a gentle boil. Add the quartered onion, chopped carrots, celery, and parsley. Season with salt and pepper. Let the broth simmer for about 10-15 minutes, allowing the flavors to meld.

Carefully add the gondhi to the simmering broth. Reduce the heat and let them cook gently for about 20-30 minutes. The gondhi should be cooked through and tender.

Before serving, you can add a squeeze of lemon juice to the broth for an added zesty flavor.

Serve the gondhi in bowls, ladling the broth and some vegetables into each bowl. Each dumpling should be a perfect blend of the ground chicken's richness and the chickpea flour's nuttiness, complemented by the aromatic spices.

There you have Persian Gondhi, a dish that's both comforting and flavorful. This meal is perfect for a cozy family dinner or a special occasion, showcasing the depth and variety of Persian cuisine. Enjoy the warm, soothing broth and the delightful dumplings, a culinary experience that's sure to please. Nooshe jan!

Enjoy

42. Australian Meat Pie Dumplings

Today, we're taking a creative twist on two beloved dishes with Australian Meat Pie Dumplings. This recipe brings the hearty and comforting flavors of a classic Australian meat pie into the fun and shareable form of dumplings. It's a perfect fusion for those who love the deep, savory flavors of a meat pie but want the convenience and novelty of a dumpling. Let's get started and bring this innovative dish to life.

Prep: 60 min. Cook: 30 min. Ready in: 1 h. 30 min. Servings: 4

Ingredients:

For the Filling:

1 tablespoon olive oil
1 pound ground beef
1 onion, finely chopped
2 cloves garlic, minced
1 carrot, finely diced
2 tablespoons all-purpose flour
1 tablespoon tomato paste
1 cup beef broth
1 teaspoon Worcestershire sauce
Salt and pepper, to taste
Fresh thyme, chopped

For the Dumplings:

Store-bought dumpling wrappers (or make your own using a basic dumpling dough recipe)

Cooking Directions:

Start with the filling. Heat olive oil in a large skillet over medium heat. Add the ground beef and cook until browned. Drain any excess fat.

Add the chopped onion, garlic, and carrot to the beef. Cook until the vegetables are softened.

Sprinkle the flour over the beef mixture and stir to combine. Add the tomato paste, beef broth, and Worcestershire sauce. Let the mixture simmer until it thickens into a gravy-like consistency. Season with salt, pepper, and fresh thyme. Remove from heat and let it cool.

Prepare the dumpling wrappers. If using store-bought, make sure they're thawed if frozen. If making your own dough, roll it out thinly and cut it into circles.

Place a spoonful of the meat filling in the center of each dumpling wrapper. Moisten the edges of the wrapper with water, fold it over the filling to form a half-moon shape, and press the edges to seal.

To cook the dumplings, you can either steam, boil, or pan-fry them. For steaming, place the dumplings in a steamer lined with parchment paper and steam for about 10 minutes. For boiling, drop them into a pot of boiling water and cook until they float to the surface. For pan-frying, heat some oil in a skillet and fry the dumplings until golden brown on both sides.

Serve the Australian Meat Pie Dumplings hot, with ketchup or another dipping sauce of your choice. They should offer the comforting flavors of a meat pie with the enjoyable texture of a dumpling.

And there you have Australian Meat Pie Dumplings, a creative and tasty fusion that's sure to please any crowd. Whether you're hosting a party, a family dinner, or just looking for a fun cooking project, these dumplings are a fantastic choice. Enjoy the blend of traditional meat pie flavors in the convenient form of a dumpling, a true testament to the versatility of comfort food.

Enjoy

43. New Zealand Seafood Pie

Today, we're diving into the culinary delights of New Zealand with their Seafood Pie. This dish celebrates the bounty of the sea, showcasing a variety of seafood in a creamy, rich sauce, all encased in a beautifully crisp pastry. It's a luxurious and comforting dish, perfect for seafood lovers and ideal for special occasions or a sumptuous family meal.

Prep: 60 min. Cook: 45 min. Ready in: 1 h. 45 min. Servings: 4

Ingredients:

For the Pastry:

2 cups all-purpose flour
1/2 cup cold butter, cubed
1/4 cup ice water
1 teaspoon salt

For the Seafood Filling:

1 tablespoon olive oil
1 onion, finely chopped
2 cloves garlic, minced
1 cup fish fillet (like cod or snapper), cubed
1 cup shrimp, peeled and deveined
1/2 cup mussels, cleaned and removed from shells
1/2 cup scallops
1 cup heavy cream
1/2 cup white wine
1 tablespoon Dijon mustard
1 tablespoon fresh parsley, chopped
Salt and pepper, to taste
Lemon juice, to taste

Cooking Directions:

Begin by making the pastry. In a large bowl, mix the flour and salt. Rub the cold butter into the flour using your fingertips until the mixture resembles coarse breadcrumbs. Gradually add ice water and mix until a dough forms. Wrap the dough in plastic wrap and chill in the refrigerator for about 30 minutes.

For the filling, heat olive oil in a large skillet over medium heat. Sauté the onion and garlic until soft and translucent. Add the cubed fish, shrimp, mussels, and scallops. Cook for a few minutes until just starting to turn opaque.

Pour in the white wine and let it reduce slightly, then add the heavy cream and Dijon mustard. Simmer gently until the sauce thickens. Season with salt, pepper, and a squeeze of lemon juice. Stir in the chopped parsley. Remove from heat and let it cool slightly.

Preheat your oven to 375°F (190°C).

Roll out the chilled pastry dough on a floured surface. Line a pie dish with the pastry, trimming any excess. Pour the seafood filling into the pastry shell.

Roll out the remaining dough to create a top for the pie. Place it over the filling, pressing the edges to seal. Make a few slits in the top to allow steam to escape.

Bake the pie in the preheated oven for about 45 minutes, or until the pastry is golden brown and the filling is bubbling.

Serve the New Zealand Seafood Pie warm. Each slice should offer a mix of flaky pastry and a rich, creamy seafood filling, a true celebration of ocean flavors.

And there you have it, New Zealand Seafood Pie, a dish that brings the essence of New Zealand's seas to your dining table. This pie is a wonderful way to enjoy a variety of seafood, all wrapped in a comforting, buttery pastry. It's perfect for impressing guests or indulging in a special family meal. Enjoy the depth of flavors and the joy of sharing this delightful dish.

Enjoy

44. Chocolate & Cherry Dumplings

Indulge in a dessert that marries the indulgence of chocolate with the natural sweetness of cherries. Chocolate & Cherry Dumplings are a delightful treat, perfect for those who love a touch of elegance in their sweets. The combination of soft, chocolatey dough and juicy cherries creates a dessert that's both comforting and sophisticated.

Prep:60 min. Cook: 25 min. Ready in: 1 h. 25 min. Servings: 4

Ingredients:

For the Dumplings:

2 cups all-purpose flour
1/4 cup cocoa powder
1/4 cup sugar
2 teaspoons baking powder
1/2 teaspoon salt
4 tablespoons cold unsalted butter, cubed
3/4 cup milk

For the Filling:

1 cup cherries, pitted and halved (fresh or frozen)
1/2 cup chocolate chips
For the Sauce:
2 cups water
1 cup sugar
2 tablespoons cherry liqueur or cherry juice
Additional chocolate chips for garnish

Cooking Directions:

Start by making the dough for the dumplings. In a large mixing bowl, whisk together the flour, cocoa powder, sugar, baking powder, and salt. Add the cubed butter, using your fingers or a pastry cutter to work it into the dry ingredients until the mixture resembles coarse crumbs. Gradually stir in the milk to form a soft dough.

For the filling, mix the cherries and chocolate chips in a bowl.

On a lightly floured surface, roll out the dough to about 1/4-inch thickness. Cut it into squares or circles.

Place a small amount of the cherry and chocolate chip mixture in the center of each dough piece. Moisten the edges of the dough with water, fold it over the filling, and press to seal.

Prepare the sauce by combining water, sugar, and cherry liqueur or juice in a large skillet. Bring it to a simmer.

Carefully place the dumplings in the simmering sauce. Cover and cook for about 20-25 minutes, or until the dumplings are puffed up and cooked through.

Serve the dumplings warm, drizzled with some of the cherry sauce and garnished with additional chocolate chips.

There you have Chocolate & Cherry Dumplings, a dessert that's as delightful to eat as it is to present. Enjoy these sweet, chocolate-infused dumplings with their burst of cherry flavor, perfect for a cozy evening treat or a special dessert after a meal. The combination of textures and flavors is sure to bring smiles to your table.

___Enjoy___

45. Mango & Sticky Rice Dumplings

Today, we're creating a fusion dessert that blends the sweet, tropical flavors of Southeast Asia with the traditional format of a dumpling. Mango & Sticky Rice Dumplings are a novel way to enjoy the classic combination of mango and sticky rice, perfect for those who appreciate inventive and delightful desserts. Let's bring this unique and tasty treat to life.

Prep: 60 min. Cook: 30 min. Ready in: 1 h. 30 min. Servings: 4

Ingredients:

For the Sticky Rice:

1 cup glutinous rice (also known as sticky rice), soaked for at least 1 hour
1 cup coconut milk
1/2 cup sugar
1/2 teaspoon salt

For the Filling:

1 large ripe mango, peeled and diced
Optional: Toasted sesame seeds or coconut flakes for garnish

For the Dumpling Wrapper:

Store-bought dumpling wrappers or homemade rice flour wrappers

Cooking Directions:

Start by preparing the sticky rice. Drain the soaked rice and steam it until it's tender, which should take about 20 minutes. While the rice is steaming, heat the coconut milk in a saucepan with the sugar and salt, stirring until the sugar is dissolved. Once the rice is cooked, mix it with the sweetened coconut milk and let it cool to room temperature. The rice should be sweet and creamy.

Prepare the mango filling by dicing the mango into small cubes.

Lay out the dumpling wrappers on a clean surface. If you're making homemade wrappers, ensure they are rolled out thinly.

Place a spoonful of the sticky rice mixture onto the center of each wrapper. Add a few pieces of diced mango on top of the rice.

Moisten the edges of the wrapper with water, then fold and seal the dumplings, making sure they are well closed to prevent the filling from leaking out during cooking.

To cook the dumplings, steam them in a bamboo steamer or a regular steamer for about 10-15 minutes, or until the wrappers become translucent.

Serve the Mango & Sticky Rice Dumplings warm or at room temperature, garnished with toasted sesame seeds or coconut flakes if desired.

And there you have it, Mango & Sticky Rice Dumplings, a dessert that's sure to delight with its combination of sweet, tropical flavors and comforting texture. This dish is perfect for a unique dessert offering at gatherings or a special treat for yourself and your family. Enjoy the harmonious blend of mango and sticky rice in each bite of these delectable dumplings.

Enjoy

46. Red Bean Bao

Today, we're venturing into the realm of East Asian culinary tradition with Red Bean Bao. These steamed buns are a beloved snack or dessert in many parts of Asia, known for their tender texture and sweet filling. The process of making bao is both therapeutic and rewarding, resulting in a delightful treat that's perfect for any time of day. Let's begin the journey of creating these soft, pillowy buns filled with sweet red bean paste.

Prep: 2 h. Cook: 15 min. Ready in: 2 h. 15 min. Servings: 4

Ingredients:

For the Dough:

2 cups all-purpose flour

1/4 cup sugar

1 tablespoon baking powder

1/2 cup warm water

1 teaspoon active dry yeast

1 tablespoon vegetable oil

For the Red Bean Filling:

1 cup red bean paste (available at Asian grocery stores or homemade)

Cooking Directions:

Begin by preparing the bao dough. Dissolve the yeast in warm water with a pinch of sugar, and let it sit for about 10 minutes until frothy.

In a large bowl, combine the flour, sugar, and baking powder. Add the yeast mixture and vegetable oil and knead the dough until it's smooth and elastic. If the dough is too sticky, add a little more flour.

Cover the dough with a damp cloth and let it rise in a warm place for about 1 to 1.5 hours, or until it doubles in size.

Once the dough has risen, punch it down and knead it briefly. Divide the dough into small equal-sized balls.

Roll out each ball into a flat circle, about 4 inches in diameter. Place a spoonful of red bean paste in the center of each circle.

Gather the edges of the dough circle around the filling, pinching them together at the top to seal the bun.

Prepare your steamer by lining it with parchment paper or cabbage leaves. Place the buns in the steamer, ensuring they are not touching as they will expand during cooking.

Steam the buns over medium-high heat for about 15 minutes, or until they are puffed and the dough is cooked through.

Serve the Red Bean Bao warm, allowing the soft, fluffy texture of the buns and the sweet, creamy filling to delight your palate.

And there you have it, Red Bean Bao, a classic dish that beautifully showcases the simplicity and elegance of East Asian desserts. These buns are perfect for a snack, a dessert, or even breakfast. Enjoy the process of making them and the joy of sharing these warm, comforting treats with friends and family.

Enjoy

47. Sweet Ricotta Dumplings with Raspberry Sauce

Indulge in the sweet and sumptuous world of dessert dumplings with this recipe for Sweet Ricotta Dumplings with Raspberry Sauce. This dessert is a celebration of simple yet exquisite flavors, blending the creamy texture of ricotta with the fresh, fruity burst of raspberries. It's an elegant and satisfying dish, perfect for a special occasion or a treat-yourself moment.

Prep: 45 min. Cook: 10 min. Ready in: 55 min. Servings: 4

Ingredients:

For the Dumplings:

1 cup ricotta cheese

1/4 cup granulated sugar

1 egg

1 teaspoon vanilla extract

1/2 cup all-purpose flour, plus more for dusting

Zest of 1 lemon

A pinch of salt

For the Raspberry Sauce:

2 cups fresh raspberries

1/4 cup sugar

1 tablespoon lemon juice

1/4 cup water

Cooking Directions:

Start by making the dumpling mixture. In a bowl, combine the ricotta cheese, sugar, egg, vanilla extract, flour, lemon zest, and a pinch of salt. Mix until you have a smooth, cohesive batter. The mixture should be thick enough to hold its shape when spooned.

Let the mixture rest in the fridge for about 30 minutes to firm up, making it easier to handle.

While the dumpling mixture is resting, prepare the raspberry sauce. In a saucepan, combine the raspberries, sugar, lemon juice, and water. Bring to a simmer over medium heat and cook until the raspberries break down and the sauce thickens slightly. This should take about 10 minutes. Strain the sauce through a fine sieve to remove the seeds, then set aside to cool.

Bring a pot of water to a gentle simmer. With floured hands, form the ricotta mixture into small balls, then carefully drop them into the simmering water.

Cook the dumplings for about 5 minutes or until they float to the surface and are cooked through. Use a slotted spoon to remove them from the water and drain them well.

Serve the dumplings warm, drizzled with the raspberry sauce. The combination of the light, fluffy dumplings with the tangy, sweet sauce creates a delightful contrast of flavors and textures.

And there you have it, Sweet Ricotta Dumplings with Raspberry Sauce, a dessert that's as visually appealing as it is delicious. This dish brings a touch of elegance to your dessert table, perfect for impressing guests or simply enjoying a luxurious treat at home. Savor the blend of creamy ricotta and vibrant raspberry, a pairing that's sure to delight your taste buds.

Enjoy

48. Plum Dumplings (Szilvásgombóc)

Today, we're making Plum Dumplings, a delightful dessert that captures the essence of home-style comfort food. Known as Szilvásgombóc in some regions, these dumplings combine the earthy flavor of potato dough with the sweet and tart taste of plums. Finished with a cinnamon-sugar breadcrumb coating, they offer a wonderful combination of flavors and textures.

Prep: 20 min. Cook: 20 min. Ready in: 1 h. 50 min. Servings: 4

Ingredients:

For the Dumplings:

2 large potatoes, peeled and boiled

2 cups all-purpose flour

1 egg

A pinch of salt

8 small plums, pitted

For the Breadcrumb Topping:

1/2 cup breadcrumbs

2 tablespoons unsalted butter

2 tablespoons sugar

1 teaspoon ground cinnamon

Cooking Directions:

Begin by mashing the boiled potatoes until smooth. Let them cool completely. Then, mix in the flour, egg, and a pinch of salt to form a dough. The dough should be soft and pliable but not too sticky.

Divide the dough into 8 equal portions. Flatten each portion in your hand and place a pitted plum in the center. Wrap the dough around the plum, completely encasing it, and form into a smooth ball.

Bring a large pot of salted water to a boil. Carefully add the dumplings and cook them for about 15-20 minutes, or until they rise to the surface and are cooked through.

While the dumplings are cooking, prepare the breadcrumb topping. Melt the butter in a pan, add the breadcrumbs, and toast them until golden brown. Stir in the sugar and cinnamon.

Once the dumplings are cooked, remove them with a slotted spoon and roll them in the spiced breadcrumb mixture until well coated.

Serve the Plum Dumplings warm. Each bite should offer the comforting texture of the potato dough, the burst of flavor from the plum, and the sweet crunch of the breadcrumb coating.

And there you have it, Plum Dumplings, a dessert that is as comforting as it is delicious. This dish is perfect for a family gathering or a cozy night in, offering a sweet and satisfying end to any meal. Enjoy these traditional dumplings and let their homey flavors and aromas bring warmth to your table.

Enjoy

49. Coconut Dumplings

Today, we're crafting a dessert that brings the essence of tropical paradise to your table with Coconut Dumplings. These dumplings are a delightful blend of coconut flavor and a soft, pillowy texture, served with a sweet and creamy coconut sauce. It's a simple yet exotic dessert that's perfect for any coconut enthusiast.

Prep: 30 min. Cook: 15 min. Ready in: 45 min. Servings: 4

Ingredients:

For the Dumplings:

1 cup all-purpose flour

1/2 cup desiccated coconut

1/4 cup sugar

1 teaspoon baking powder

A pinch of salt

1/2 cup coconut milk

1 egg

For the Coconut Sauce:

1 cup coconut milk

1/4 cup sugar

1 teaspoon vanilla extract

1 tablespoon cornstarch, dissolved in 2 tablespoons water

Cooking Directions:

Begin by preparing the dough for the dumplings. In a mixing bowl, combine the flour, desiccated coconut, sugar, baking powder, and a pinch of salt. In another bowl, whisk together the coconut milk and egg. Gradually add the wet ingredients to the dry ingredients, stirring until a soft dough forms.

Bring a large pot of water to a gentle boil.

Using two spoons or a small ice cream scoop, form the dough into small balls and drop them into the boiling water. Cook the dumplings for about 10-15 minutes, or until they float to the surface and are cooked through.

While the dumplings are cooking, prepare the coconut sauce. In a saucepan, combine the coconut milk, sugar, and vanilla extract. Bring to a simmer over medium heat. Add the dissolved cornstarch and stir continuously until the sauce thickens slightly.

Once the dumplings are cooked, remove them from the water with a slotted spoon and transfer them to serving dishes.

Pour the warm coconut sauce over the dumplings and serve immediately.

And there you have it, Coconut Dumplings, a dessert that's both comforting and exotic. These dumplings, with their tender texture and rich coconut flavor, are a perfect way to end any meal on a sweet note. Enjoy this tropical delight and let the flavors transport you to a beachside paradise.

Enjoy

50. Fried Banana Dumplings

Let's dive into a sweet and indulgent treat with Fried Banana Dumplings. This dessert is perfect for banana lovers and anyone who enjoys a combination of fruity flavors with a crispy texture. These dumplings are simple to make yet offer a delightful dessert experience, perfect for a cozy evening or a special occasion.

Prep: 30 min. Cook: 15 min. Ready in: 45 min. Servings: 4

Ingredients:

For the Dumpling Dough:

2 cups all-purpose flour
1/4 cup sugar
1/2 teaspoon baking powder
A pinch of salt
1/2 cup water (or as needed)
1 egg, beaten

For the Filling:

2 ripe bananas, sliced
1 teaspoon ground cinnamon
2 tablespoons brown sugar

For Frying:

Vegetable oil, for deep frying

For Serving:

Powdered sugar or honey for drizzling
Optional: scoop of vanilla ice cream

Cooking Directions:

Start by preparing the dumpling dough. In a large bowl, mix together the flour, sugar, baking powder, and a pinch of salt. Add the beaten egg and gradually mix in enough water to form a smooth, pliable dough.

In a small bowl, toss the sliced bananas with cinnamon and brown sugar. This adds a lovely spiced sweetness to the bananas.

On a floured surface, roll out the dough to about 1/4-inch thickness. Cut it into squares or circles.

Place a few slices of the banana mixture in the center of each dough piece. Fold the dough over the filling to create a half-moon shape and press the edges to seal them. You can use a fork to crimp the edges for a decorative look.

Heat vegetable oil in a deep fryer or a large deep pan to 350°F (175°C). Fry the dumplings in batches, turning them occasionally, until they are golden brown and crispy.

Drain the fried dumplings on paper towels to remove excess oil.

Serve the Fried Banana Dumplings warm, drizzled with powdered sugar or honey. For an extra indulgent treat, serve them with a scoop of vanilla ice cream on the side.

There you have it, Fried Banana Dumplings, a delightful dessert that's sure to please anyone with a sweet tooth. These dumplings are a fantastic way to enjoy the comforting flavors of banana in a fun and delicious package. Whether you're serving them at a gathering or enjoying them as a special treat, they're sure to be a hit.

Enjoy

51. Nutella and Marshmallow Dumplings

Indulge in a delightful fusion of flavors with Nutella and Marshmallow Dumplings. This dessert is a playful and irresistible treat, combining the creamy hazelnut spread with the classic sweetness of marshmallows. Wrapped in a light, fluffy dough and deep-fried to golden perfection, these dumplings are perfect for a special occasion or as a treat to satisfy your sweet cravings.

Prep: 30 min. Cook: 10 min. Ready in: 40 min. Servings: 4

Ingredients:

For the Dough:

2 cups all-purpose flour
1/4 cup sugar
1/2 teaspoon baking powder
A pinch of salt
1/2 cup milk
2 tablespoons unsalted butter, melted

For the Filling:

Nutella (about 1/2 cup)
Mini marshmallows

For Frying:

Vegetable oil, for deep frying

For Serving:

Powdered sugar for dusting
Optional: Additional Nutella or chocolate sauce for dipping

Cooking Directions:

Begin with the dough. In a mixing bowl, combine the flour, sugar, baking powder, and a pinch of salt. Stir in the milk and melted butter, mixing until a soft dough forms. Knead the dough gently until it's smooth and elastic.

Roll out the dough on a floured surface to about 1/4-inch thickness. Cut it into squares or circles using a cookie cutter or a knife.

Spoon a small amount of Nutella in the center of each dough piece, and add a few mini marshmallows on top of the Nutella.

Fold the dough over the filling to create a half-moon shape and press the edges to seal them securely. Ensure the dumplings are sealed well to prevent the filling from leaking out during frying.

Heat vegetable oil in a deep fryer or a large deep pan to 350°F (175°C). Fry the dumplings in batches, turning them occasionally, until they are golden brown and crispy.

Drain the fried dumplings on paper towels to remove excess oil.

Serve the Nutella and Marshmallow Dumplings warm, dusted with powdered sugar. Offer additional Nutella or chocolate sauce for dipping, if desired.

There you have it, Nutella and Marshmallow Dumplings, a heavenly dessert that's as delightful to eat as it is to make. These dumplings are a perfect treat for gatherings, parties, or simply as a decadent dessert to enjoy at home. Relish the rich, chocolaty flavor paired with the soft, sweet marshmallows in every bite.

Enjoy

52. Blueberry Pierogi

Today, we're putting a sweet spin on a classic Eastern European dish with Blueberry Pierogi. These dumplings combine the tender, chewy texture of pierogi dough with the natural sweetness and slight tartness of blueberries. It's a perfect dish for those who enjoy a sweet take on traditional savory recipes.

Prep: 60 min. Cook: 15 min. Ready in: 1 h. 15 min. Servings: 4

Ingredients:

For the Dough:

2 cups all-purpose flour
1/2 teaspoon salt
1 egg
1/2 cup water

For the Filling:

1 cup fresh blueberries
2 tablespoons sugar
1 teaspoon lemon zest
1 tablespoon lemon juice

For Serving:

Melted butter
Additional sugar, for sprinkling
Sour cream or whipped cream (optional)

Cooking Directions:

Begin by making the pierogi dough. In a large bowl, mix together the flour and salt. Make a well in the center and add the egg and water. Mix until a dough forms, then knead on a floured surface until smooth and elastic. Let the dough rest for about 30 minutes.

For the filling, gently toss the blueberries with sugar, lemon zest, and lemon juice. Be careful not to crush the berries.

Roll out the dough on a floured surface until it's about 1/8-inch thick. Use a round cutter or a glass to cut circles from the dough.

Place a spoonful of the blueberry filling on each dough circle. Fold the dough over to form a half-moon shape and press the edges to seal. Ensure the edges are well sealed to keep the filling inside during cooking.

Bring a large pot of salted water to a boil. Cook the pierogi in batches, being careful not to overcrowd the pot. They are done when they float to the surface, about 3 to 4 minutes.

Serve the Blueberry Pierogi warm, drizzled with melted butter and sprinkled with sugar. They can also be enjoyed with a side of sour cream or whipped cream for added richness.

And there you have it, Blueberry Pierogi, a sweet and delightful variation of a beloved classic. These dumplings offer a burst of berry flavor in every bite, making them a perfect treat for dessert or a special snack. Enjoy the fusion of traditional dough and sweet, tangy blueberries in this unique and tasty dish.

Enjoy

53. Almond and Orange Blossom Dumplings

Indulge in the delicate and fragrant world of Almond and Orange Blossom Dumplings. This dessert is a celebration of subtle yet distinct flavors, creating a sophisticated and refined taste experience. The combination of almond and orange blossom imparts a unique, floral sweetness that makes these dumplings a delightful end to any meal.

Prep: 45 min. Cook: 20 min. Ready in: 1 h. 5 min. Servings: 4

Ingredients:

For the Dumplings:

1 1/2 cups all-purpose flour
1/2 cup ground almonds (almond meal)
1/4 cup sugar
1/2 teaspoon salt
1 egg, beaten
1/4 cup unsalted butter, melted
1/4 cup milk
1 teaspoon orange blossom water

For the Syrup:

1 cup sugar
1/2 cup water
1 tablespoon orange blossom water
Zest of 1 orange
For Garnish:
Sliced almonds, toasted
Powdered sugar

Cooking Directions:

Begin by making the dough for the dumplings. In a large bowl, combine the flour, ground almonds, sugar, and salt. Mix in the beaten egg, melted butter, milk, and orange blossom water, stirring until a smooth dough forms. Let the dough rest for about 20 minutes.

While the dough is resting, prepare the syrup. In a saucepan, combine the sugar, water, and orange zest. Bring it to a simmer over medium heat, stirring until the sugar dissolves. Add the orange blossom water and simmer for another 5 minutes. Remove from heat and set aside.

Roll the dough into small balls, about the size of a walnut.

Bring a pot of water to a gentle boil. Carefully drop the dumplings into the water and cook them for about 10-15 minutes, or until they rise to the surface and are cooked through.

Using a slotted spoon, transfer the cooked dumplings to the syrup. Let them soak for a few minutes, gently turning to coat them evenly.

To serve, place the dumplings on a serving plate, drizzle with some of the syrup, and garnish with toasted sliced almonds and a dusting of powdered sugar.

There you have Almond and Orange Blossom Dumplings, a dessert that's as beautiful to look at as it is to savor. These dumplings are a testament to the elegance of combining simple ingredients to create a dish with depth and sophistication. Enjoy these fragrant, sweet treats as a perfect conclusion to a special meal or as a refined indulgence on their own.

Enjoy

54. Spinach and Ricotta Dumplings

Today, we're making Spinach and Ricotta Dumplings, a dish that beautifully balances simplicity and flavor. These dumplings are a testament to the comfort and versatility of vegetarian cooking, showcasing how a few ingredients can create something both nourishing and delicious. Let's enjoy the process of making these delightful dumplings.

Prep: 30 min. Cook: 20 min. Ready in: 50 min. Servings: 4

Ingredients:

For the Dumplings:

2 cups fresh spinach leaves
1 cup ricotta cheese
1/2 cup grated Parmesan cheese
2 eggs, beaten
3/4 cup all-purpose flour, plus more for dusting
Salt and pepper, to taste
Nutmeg, to taste

For the Sauce:

2 tablespoons unsalted butter
1 clove garlic, minced
1/2 cup heavy cream
Salt and pepper, to taste
Additional grated Parmesan cheese, for garnish
Fresh basil leaves, for garnish

Cooking Directions:

Start by preparing the spinach. Cook the spinach leaves in boiling water for a few minutes until wilted. Drain and squeeze out as much water as possible. Chop the spinach finely.

In a mixing bowl, combine the chopped spinach, ricotta cheese, Parmesan cheese, beaten eggs, flour, salt, pepper, and a touch of nutmeg. Mix until well combined. The mixture should be thick enough to form into balls.

Bring a large pot of salted water to a gentle boil.

With floured hands, form the spinach and ricotta mixture into small, bite-sized balls. Gently drop the dumplings into the boiling water. Cook them until they float to the surface, indicating they are done, about 3-5 minutes.

While the dumplings are cooking, prepare the sauce. In a skillet, melt the butter over medium heat. Add the minced garlic and sauté until fragrant. Pour in the heavy cream, season with salt and pepper, and let it simmer until slightly thickened.

Using a slotted spoon, transfer the cooked dumplings into the skillet with the sauce. Gently toss to coat the dumplings.

Serve the Spinach and Ricotta Dumplings warm, garnished with additional Parmesan cheese and fresh basil leaves.

Enjoy your Spinach and Ricotta Dumplings, a dish that's both comforting and elegant. These dumplings are a wonderful showcase of how simple ingredients can come together to create a dish that's full of flavor and texture. Perfect for a cozy dinner or a special occasion, they're sure to satisfy both vegetarians and meat-eaters alike.

Enjoy

55. Edamame & Truffle Dumplings

Today, we're diving into a culinary delight with Edamame & Truffle Dumplings, a dish that brings together the freshness of edamame beans with the rich, earthy flavor of truffle. This recipe is a fusion of Asian-inspired flavors and luxurious ingredients, creating a dining experience that's both elegant and exciting.

Prep: 45 min. Cook: 15 min. Ready in: 1 h. Servings: 4

Ingredients:

For the Dumplings:

2 cups shelled edamame, cooked and cooled

1 tablespoon truffle oil

2 cloves garlic, minced

1 inch ginger, grated

1/4 cup green onions, finely chopped

Salt and pepper, to taste

Wonton wrappers

For the Dipping Sauce:

1/4 cup soy sauce

1 tablespoon rice vinegar

1 teaspoon sesame oil

1 teaspoon honey

1/2 teaspoon chili flakes (optional)

Additional truffle oil for drizzling (optional)

Cooking Directions:

Begin by preparing the dumpling filling. In a food processor, blend the cooked edamame until it forms a coarse paste. Transfer to a mixing bowl.

Add the truffle oil, minced garlic, grated ginger, and green onions to the edamame paste. Season with salt and pepper. Mix well to combine all the flavors. The mixture should be fragrant with a hint of truffle.

Lay out the wonton wrappers on a clean surface. Place a small spoonful of the edamame filling in the center of each wrapper.

Moisten the edges of the wrappers with water. Fold the wrappers over the filling to form a triangle or your desired shape, pressing the edges to seal them securely.

Bring a pot of water to a gentle boil, or prepare a steamer. Cook the dumplings in batches, either by boiling or steaming, for about 3-5 minutes, or until they are translucent and the filling is heated through.

While the dumplings are cooking, prepare the dipping sauce. In a small bowl, combine soy sauce, rice vinegar, sesame oil, honey, and chili flakes. Mix well.

Serve the Edamame & Truffle Dumplings warm with the dipping sauce on the side. For an added touch of luxury, drizzle a bit more truffle oil over the dumplings.

Enjoy your Edamame & Truffle Dumplings, a dish that's sure to impress with its blend of unique flavors and textures. These dumplings are perfect for a special occasion, a gourmet gathering, or when you simply crave something extraordinary. Savor each bite and the exquisite combination of edamame and truffle in this delightful dish.

Enjoy

56. Vegan Jackfruit 'Pork' Dumplings

Today, we're embracing the versatility of plant-based cooking with Vegan Jackfruit 'Pork' Dumplings. This recipe is a fantastic way to enjoy the flavors and textures of traditional dumplings in a completely vegan form. Jackfruit, with its unique texture, makes an excellent substitute for pork, offering a satisfying and flavorful experience.

Prep: 60 min. Cook: 20 min. Ready in: 1 h. 20 min. Servings: 4

Ingredients:

For the Dumplings:

2 cups young green jackfruit (canned, drained, and rinsed)

1 tablespoon sesame oil

1 small onion, finely chopped

2 cloves garlic, minced

1 inch ginger, grated

2 tablespoons soy sauce

1 teaspoon rice vinegar

1 teaspoon smoked paprika

1/4 cup green onions, finely chopped

Salt and pepper, to taste

Vegan dumpling wrappers

For Cooking:

Vegetable oil, for frying

Water, for steaming

For the Dipping Sauce:

1/4 cup soy sauce

1 tablespoon rice vinegar

1 teaspoon sesame oil

1/2 teaspoon chili flakes (optional)

1 teaspoon agave syrup or sugar

Cooking Directions:

Start by preparing the jackfruit filling. Shred the jackfruit into small pieces, resembling the texture of pulled pork.

Heat sesame oil in a pan over medium heat. Add the onion, garlic, and ginger, sautéing until fragrant and the onions are translucent.

Add the shredded jackfruit, soy sauce, rice vinegar, and smoked paprika to the pan. Cook for about 5-7 minutes, stirring occasionally, until the jackfruit is well-coated with the seasonings and heated through. Stir in the green onions, and season with salt and pepper. Remove from heat and let the mixture cool.

Lay out the vegan dumpling wrappers on a clean surface. Place a small amount of the jackfruit filling in the center of each wrapper.

Moisten the edges of the wrapper with water. Fold the wrapper over the filling to form a half-moon shape, pressing the edges to seal them securely.

To cook the dumplings, heat a small amount of vegetable oil in a skillet. Place the dumplings in the skillet and cook until the bottoms are golden brown. Add a small amount of water to the skillet (about 1/4 cup), and cover immediately to steam the dumplings. Cook until the water has evaporated and the dumplings are tender.

While the dumplings are cooking, prepare the dipping sauce. Combine soy sauce, rice vinegar, sesame oil, chili flakes, and agave syrup or sugar in a small bowl.

Serve the Vegan Jackfruit 'Pork' Dumplings hot, with the dipping sauce on the side for a delicious and satisfying plant-based meal.

Enjoy your Vegan Jackfruit 'Pork' Dumplings, a dish that showcases the incredible possibilities of vegan cooking. These dumplings are not only a testament to culinary creativity but also offer a delightful and flavorful experience that can be enjoyed by everyone, regardless of dietary preferences. Savor the flavors and share this innovative dish with friends and family.

Enjoy

57. Cauliflower and Potato Samosas

Embrace the flavors of India with these Cauliflower and Potato Samosas. This recipe is a delightful way to enjoy the traditional taste of samosas with a vegan filling. The combination of spiced cauliflower and potatoes makes for a hearty and flavorful snack, perfect for any occasion.

Prep: 60 min. Cook: 30 min. Ready in: 1 h. 30 min. Servings: 4

Ingredients:

For the Samosa Dough:

2 cups all-purpose flour
1/4 cup vegetable oil
1/2 teaspoon salt
Approximately 1/2 cup water

For the Filling:
1 tablespoon vegetable oil
1 small head cauliflower, finely chopped
2 medium potatoes, peeled and finely diced
1 small onion, finely chopped
2 cloves garlic, minced
1 inch ginger, grated
1 teaspoon ground cumin
1 teaspoon ground coriander
1/2 teaspoon turmeric
1/2 teaspoon garam masala
1/2 teaspoon chili powder
Salt to taste
Fresh cilantro, chopped

For Frying:

Vegetable oil, for deep frying

Cooking Directions:

Start by making the dough for the samosas. In a bowl, combine the flour, salt, and oil. Gradually add water and knead into a firm dough. Cover and set aside to rest.

For the filling, heat oil in a pan. Add the onions, garlic, and ginger, sautéing until the onions are translucent. Add the cauliflower and potatoes, cooking until they are tender.

Stir in the cumin, coriander, turmeric, garam masala, chili powder, and salt. Cook for a few more minutes until the spices are well blended with the vegetables. Remove from heat and stir in the chopped cilantro. Allow the filling to cool.

Divide the dough into small balls. Roll each ball into a thin circle, then cut it in half to form two semi-circles.

Place a spoonful of the filling on one half of each semi-circle. Moisten the edges with water, fold over, and press to seal, forming a triangular shape.

Heat oil in a deep fryer or a large pan. Fry the samosas in batches until golden brown and crispy.

Serve the Cauliflower and Potato Samosas hot with chutney or ketchup. They are perfect as a snack, appetizer, or part of a larger meal.

Enjoy your Cauliflower and Potato Samosas, a vegan take on a beloved classic. These samosas offer a wonderful blend of flavors and textures, sure to be a hit whether you're serving them at a party or enjoying them as a treat. Share and savor these delightful bites, a testament to the versatility and richness of Indian cuisine.

Enjoy

58. Vegan Lentil and Mushroom Dumplings

Today, we're making Vegan Lentil and Mushroom Dumplings, a dish that perfectly showcases the delicious possibilities of plant-based ingredients. These dumplings are packed with flavor and offer a satisfying texture, making them a fantastic choice for both vegans and non-vegans alike.

__Prep: 60 min. Cook: 20 min. Ready in: 1 h. 20 min. Servings: 4__

Ingredients:

For the Dumplings:

Vegan dumpling wrappers (store-bought or homemade)
For the Filling:
1 cup brown lentils, cooked and drained
1 tablespoon olive oil
1 small onion, finely chopped
2 cloves garlic, minced
1 cup mushrooms, finely chopped
1 teaspoon soy sauce
1 teaspoon smoked paprika
Salt and pepper, to taste
Fresh herbs (like thyme or parsley), chopped

For the Dipping Sauce:

1/4 cup soy sauce
1 tablespoon rice vinegar
1 teaspoon sesame oil
1/2 teaspoon chili flakes (optional)
1 teaspoon maple syrup or sugar

Cooking Directions:

Start by preparing the filling. Heat olive oil in a pan over medium heat. Sauté the onion and garlic until the onion is translucent. Add the chopped mushrooms and cook until they release their moisture and begin to brown.

Stir in the cooked lentils, soy sauce, smoked paprika, and a generous sprinkle of salt and pepper. Cook for a few more minutes, allowing the flavors to meld together. Remove from heat and stir in the chopped herbs. Let the mixture cool.

Place a small spoonful of the lentil and mushroom filling in the center of each dumpling wrapper. Moisten the edges of the wrapper with water, fold it over the filling, and press to seal, forming a half-moon shape. Make sure the edges are tightly sealed to prevent the filling from escaping during cooking.

To cook the dumplings, you can either steam, boil, or pan-fry them. For steaming, place the dumplings in a steamer lined with parchment paper and steam for about 10 minutes. For boiling, drop them into boiling water and cook until they float to the surface. For pan-frying, heat some oil in a skillet and fry the dumplings until golden brown on both sides.

While the dumplings are cooking, prepare the dipping sauce by mixing together soy sauce, rice vinegar, sesame oil, chili flakes, and maple syrup or sugar.

Serve the Vegan Lentil and Mushroom Dumplings hot, with the dipping sauce on the side.

Enjoy your Vegan Lentil and Mushroom Dumplings, a delightful and nutritious dish that's perfect for any occasion. Whether you're hosting a dinner party, looking for a tasty snack, or simply exploring vegan cuisine, these dumplings are sure to impress with their rich flavors and satisfying texture.

Enjoy

59. Sweet Potato and Black Bean Empanadas

Today, we're making Sweet Potato and Black Bean Empanadas, a delightful fusion of flavors that's sure to please any palate. These empanadas are a fantastic way to enjoy a vegetarian meal, combining nutritious ingredients with a burst of flavor in every bite.

Prep: 60 min. Cook: 25 min. Ready in: 1 h. 25 min. Servings: 4

Ingredients:

For the Dough:

2 cups all-purpose flour
1/2 teaspoon salt
1/2 cup unsalted butter, chilled and cubed
1/3 cup ice water

For the Filling:

1 large sweet potato, peeled and diced
1 tablespoon olive oil
1 small onion, finely chopped
1 clove garlic, minced
1 cup black beans, cooked and drained
1 teaspoon ground cumin
1/2 teaspoon smoked paprika
Salt and pepper, to taste
Fresh cilantro, chopped

For Baking:

1 egg, beaten (for egg wash)

Cooking Directions:

Begin by preparing the dough. In a large bowl, mix the flour and salt. Add the chilled, cubed butter and use a pastry cutter or your fingers to incorporate it until the mixture resembles coarse crumbs. Gradually add the ice water, mixing until a dough forms. Wrap the dough in plastic wrap and chill in the refrigerator for at least 30 minutes.

For the filling, cook the diced sweet potato in boiling water until tender, about 15 minutes. Drain and set aside.

In a pan, heat the olive oil over medium heat. Sauté the onion and garlic until the onion is translucent. Add the cooked sweet potato and black beans, then season with cumin, smoked paprika, salt, and pepper. Cook for a few more minutes, then remove from heat and stir in the chopped cilantro. Let the mixture cool.

Preheat your oven to 375°F (190°C).

Roll out the chilled dough on a floured surface. Cut it into circles using a round cutter or a glass.

Spoon a portion of the sweet potato and black bean filling onto one half of each dough circle. Fold the dough over the filling to create a half-moon shape, pressing the edges to seal. Crimp the edges with a fork for a decorative touch.

Place the empanadas on a baking sheet lined with parchment paper. Brush the tops with the beaten egg for a golden finish.

Bake the empanadas for about 25 minutes, or until they are golden brown and crispy.

Serve the Sweet Potato and Black Bean Empanadas warm, possibly accompanied by a side of salsa or sour cream.

Enjoy your Sweet Potato and Black Bean Empanadas, a dish that's not only delicious but also packed with wholesome ingredients. These empanadas are perfect for a family meal, a friendly gathering, or as a tasty snack. The combination of sweet potato and black beans wrapped in a flaky crust is sure to be a hit with everyone.

Enjoy

60. Zucchini & Corn Dumplings

Today, we're making Zucchini & Corn Dumplings, a light and flavorful dish that's perfect for a summer meal or as a unique vegetarian option. The combination of zucchini and corn creates a dumpling that's both tender and full of fresh flavors, complemented by a simple yet delicious buttery lemon sauce.

Prep: 45 min. Cook: 20 min. Ready in: 1 h. 5 min. Servings: 4

Ingredients:

For the Dumplings:
2 cups grated zucchini
1 cup corn kernels (fresh or frozen)
2 cloves garlic, minced
1/2 cup all-purpose flour
1/4 cup cornmeal
1/2 teaspoon baking powder
Salt and pepper, to taste
2 eggs, beaten
2 tablespoons olive oil

For the Sauce:
1/4 cup unsalted butter
1 tablespoon fresh lemon juice
1/4 cup grated Parmesan cheese
Fresh basil leaves, chopped
Salt and pepper, to taste

Cooking Directions:

Start by preparing the zucchini. Grate the zucchini and place it in a colander. Sprinkle with a little salt and let it sit for about 10 minutes to draw out excess moisture. Squeeze the zucchini to remove as much water as possible.

In a large bowl, combine the grated zucchini, corn kernels, and minced garlic. Add the flour, cornmeal, baking powder, salt, and pepper. Mix well.

Stir in the beaten eggs until the mixture is well combined. The mixture should hold together; if it's too wet, add a little more flour.

Heat olive oil in a large skillet over medium heat. Scoop spoonfuls of the zucchini mixture into the skillet, flattening them slightly to form small dumplings. Fry until golden brown on both sides. Remove and drain on paper towels.

For the sauce, melt the butter in a small saucepan over medium heat. Add the lemon juice, Parmesan cheese, and chopped basil. Season with salt and pepper. Stir until the sauce is smooth and the cheese has melted.

Serve the Zucchini & Corn Dumplings drizzled with the buttery lemon sauce. Garnish with extra basil leaves if desired.

Enjoy your Zucchini & Corn Dumplings, a dish that's as delightful to eat as it is simple to prepare. These dumplings offer a wonderful combination of garden-fresh zucchini and sweet corn, enhanced by the rich and tangy sauce. It's a perfect dish for a light lunch, dinner, or as an appetizing side dish.

Enjoy

61. Lobster & Corn Dumplings

Indulge in the exquisite combination of seafood and vegetables with Lobster & Corn Dumplings. This recipe offers a delightful blend of flavors and textures, perfect for those who appreciate the finer things in life. Each dumpling is a bite of luxury, showcasing the succulent taste of lobster and the natural sweetness of corn.

Prep: 60 min. Cook: 20 min. Ready in: 1 h. 20 min. Servings: 4

Ingredients:

For the Filling:
1 cup cooked lobster meat, finely chopped
1/2 cup corn kernels (fresh or frozen)
1/4 cup cream cheese, softened
2 green onions, finely chopped
1 teaspoon lemon zest
Salt and pepper, to taste
A pinch of cayenne pepper (optional)

For the Dumplings:
Store-bought or homemade dumpling wrappers

For Cooking:
Vegetable oil, for frying
Water, for steaming

For the Dipping Sauce:
1/4 cup soy sauce
1 tablespoon rice vinegar
1 teaspoon sesame oil
1/2 teaspoon honey
1/2 teaspoon grated ginger
1 clove garlic, minced

Cooking Directions:

Start by preparing the filling. In a bowl, mix together the chopped lobster meat, corn kernels, cream cheese, green onions, and lemon zest. Season with salt, pepper, and a pinch of cayenne pepper for some heat, if desired. The mixture should be well combined and flavorful.

Lay out the dumpling wrappers on a clean surface. Spoon a small amount of the lobster and corn filling into the center of each wrapper. Moisten the edges of the wrapper with water, fold it over the filling, and press to seal, forming a half-moon shape. Make sure the edges are tightly sealed to prevent the filling from leaking out during cooking.

To cook the dumplings, you can either pan-fry or steam them. For pan-frying, heat some oil in a skillet and fry the dumplings until golden brown on both sides. For steaming, place the dumplings in a steamer lined with parchment paper and steam for about 10 minutes.

While the dumplings are cooking, prepare the dipping sauce. In a small bowl, mix together soy sauce, rice vinegar, sesame oil, honey, grated ginger, and minced garlic.

Serve the Lobster & Corn Dumplings hot, with the dipping sauce on the side. Each bite should offer a burst of the rich lobster and sweet corn filling, complemented by the tangy and flavorful sauce.

Savor the luxurious taste of Lobster & Corn Dumplings, a dish that's sure to impress and delight. Whether you're hosting a dinner party or treating yourself to a gourmet meal, these dumplings provide a memorable and indulgent dining experience. Enjoy the harmony of flavors and the joy of sharing this exquisite dish.

Enjoy

62. Tuna Tartare Potstickers

Embark on a culinary adventure with Tuna Tartare Potstickers, a dish that marries the elegance of tuna tartare with the playful form of potstickers. This recipe is a wonderful choice for a sophisticated appetizer or a special snack, offering a unique blend of textures and flavors.

Prep: 45 min. Cook: 10 min. Ready in: 55 min. Servings: 4

Ingredients:

For the Tuna Tartare:
1/2 pound fresh, sushi-grade tuna, finely diced
1 avocado, finely diced
1/4 cup cucumber, finely diced
1 tablespoon soy sauce
1 teaspoon sesame oil
1 teaspoon lime juice
1 teaspoon fresh ginger, grated
1 small jalapeño, finely chopped (optional)
Salt and pepper, to taste

For the Potstickers:
Store-bought or homemade potsticker wrappers

For Cooking:
Vegetable oil, for frying
Water, for steaming

For the Dipping Sauce:
1/4 cup soy sauce
1 tablespoon rice vinegar
1 teaspoon sesame oil
1/2 teaspoon honey
1/2 teaspoon grated ginger
1 clove garlic, minced

Cooking Directions:

Begin by preparing the tuna tartare. In a bowl, mix together the diced tuna, avocado, cucumber, soy sauce, sesame oil, lime juice, grated ginger, and jalapeño (if using). Season with salt and pepper. The mixture should be flavorful and well-balanced.

Lay out the potsticker wrappers on a clean surface. Place a small spoonful of the tuna tartare mixture in the center of each wrapper.

Moisten the edges of the wrapper with water, fold it over the filling, and press to seal, forming a half-moon shape. Ensure the edges are tightly sealed.

To cook the potstickers, heat a small amount of vegetable oil in a skillet. Place the potstickers in the skillet and cook until the bottoms are golden brown. Add a small amount of water to the skillet (about 1/4 cup), and cover immediately to steam the potstickers. Cook until the water has evaporated.

While the potstickers are cooking, prepare the dipping sauce by mixing together soy sauce, rice vinegar, sesame oil, honey, grated ginger, and minced garlic.

Serve the Tuna Tartare Potstickers hot, with the dipping sauce on the side. Each potsticker should offer a fresh and flavorful bite of tuna tartare in a crispy, golden wrapper.

Enjoy your Tuna Tartare Potstickers, a creative fusion dish that's as delightful to eat as it is to present. Perfect for entertaining or as a special treat, these potstickers offer a unique and sophisticated take on traditional dumplings. Savor the fresh flavors and the joy of sharing this elegant appetizer.

Enjoy

63. Scallop & Chive Dumplings

Today, we're creating Scallop & Chive Dumplings, a dish that perfectly balances the sweetness of scallops with the subtle onion flavor of chives. This recipe is ideal for those who enjoy seafood and are looking for an elegant, yet simple-to-prepare dish.

Prep: 45 min. Cook: 10 min. Ready in: 55 min. Servings: 4

Ingredients:

For the Dumplings:
1/2 pound fresh scallops, finely chopped
1/4 cup chives, finely chopped
1 tablespoon soy sauce
1 teaspoon sesame oil
1 teaspoon grated ginger
1 clove garlic, minced
Salt and pepper, to taste
Dumpling wrappers (store-bought or homemade)

For Cooking:
Vegetable oil, for frying
Water, for steaming

For the Dipping Sauce:
1/4 cup soy sauce
1 tablespoon rice vinegar
1 teaspoon sesame oil
1/2 teaspoon sugar
A pinch of red pepper flakes (optional)

Cooking Directions:

Begin by preparing the filling. In a bowl, combine the finely chopped scallops, chives, soy sauce, sesame oil, grated ginger, and minced garlic. Season with salt and pepper. Mix well to ensure the flavors are evenly distributed throughout the filling.

Lay out the dumpling wrappers on a clean surface. Place a small amount of the scallop and chive filling in the center of each wrapper. Moisten the edges of the wrapper with water, fold it over the filling, and press to seal, forming a half-moon shape. Make sure the edges are tightly sealed to prevent the filling from leaking out during cooking.

To cook the dumplings, you can either pan-fry or steam them. For pan-frying, heat some oil in a skillet and fry the dumplings until golden brown on both sides. For steaming, place the dumplings in a steamer lined with parchment paper and steam for about 10 minutes.

While the dumplings are cooking, prepare the dipping sauce. In a small bowl, mix together soy sauce, rice vinegar, sesame oil, sugar, and red pepper flakes, if using.

Serve the Scallop & Chive Dumplings hot, with the dipping sauce on the side. Each bite should offer a burst of the rich and sweet flavor of scallops, complemented by the fresh chives and the savory dipping sauce.

Enjoy your Scallop & Chive Dumplings, a dish that's both sophisticated and satisfying. These dumplings are perfect for a special occasion or a gourmet meal at home, offering a delightful combination of flavors that seafood lovers will adore. Share and savor this elegant and delicious creation.

Enjoy

64. Crab Rangoon

Today, we're making Crab Rangoon, a delightful fusion of Eastern and Western flavors. This dish is beloved for its crispy exterior and creamy, savory filling. Perfect for parties, gatherings, or as a tasty snack, Crab Rangoon is always a crowd-pleaser.

Prep: 30 min. Cook: 10 min. Ready in: 40 min. Servings: 4

Ingredients:

For the Filling:

1 cup cooked crab meat, finely chopped

8 ounces cream cheese, softened

2 green onions, finely chopped

1 garlic clove, minced

1 teaspoon Worcestershire sauce

1 teaspoon soy sauce

Salt and pepper, to taste

For the Wontons:

Wonton wrappers

Vegetable oil, for deep frying

For the Dipping Sauce:

1/2 cup sweet and sour sauce

1 tablespoon soy sauce

1 teaspoon sesame oil

Cooking Directions:

Start by preparing the crab filling. In a bowl, combine the crab meat, cream cheese, green onions, garlic, Worcestershire sauce, and soy sauce. Season with salt and pepper. Mix well until all the ingredients are thoroughly combined.

Lay out the wonton wrappers on a clean surface. Place a small spoonful of the crab mixture in the center of each wrapper.

Moisten the edges of the wrapper with water. Bring the corners of the wrapper together above the filling, pinching the edges to seal and create a four-pointed star shape. Ensure that the wontons are well sealed to prevent the filling from leaking out during frying.

Heat vegetable oil in a deep fryer or a large deep pan to 350°F (175°C). Fry the Crab Rangoon in batches, turning them occasionally, until they are golden brown and crispy.

For the dipping sauce, mix together the sweet and sour sauce, soy sauce, and sesame oil in a small bowl.

Serve the Crab Rangoon hot, with the dipping sauce on the side. Each bite should offer a contrast of the crispy wonton wrapper with the creamy, flavorful crab filling.

There you have it, Crab Rangoon, a dish that's as fun to eat as it is to make. Enjoy these at your next gathering or whenever you're in the mood for a delicious and indulgent treat. The combination of crab and cream cheese wrapped in a crispy shell makes for an unforgettable appetizer.

Enjoy

65. Fish and Dill Pierogi

Today, we're making Fish and Dill Pierogi, a dish that brings a refreshing twist to the traditional pierogi. Combining the delicate flavor of fish with the aromatic freshness of dill, these dumplings are a delightful treat for anyone who loves seafood and enjoys exploring different variations of classic recipes.

Prep: 60 min. Cook: 30 min. Ready in: 1 h. 30 min. Servings: 4

Ingredients:

For the Dough:
2 cups all-purpose flour
1/2 teaspoon salt
1 egg
About 1/2 cup water

For the Filling:
1 pound white fish fillets (such as cod or tilapia), cooked and flaked
2 tablespoons unsalted butter
1 small onion, finely chopped
2 tablespoons fresh dill, chopped
Salt and pepper, to taste

For Serving:
Melted butter
Sour cream
Additional chopped dill for garnish

Cooking Directions:

Begin by preparing the pierogi dough. In a large bowl, mix together the flour and salt. Make a well in the center and add the egg and water. Mix until a dough forms, then knead on a floured surface until smooth and elastic. Let the dough rest for about 30 minutes.

For the filling, melt the butter in a pan over medium heat. Sauté the onion until translucent, then mix in the cooked, flaked fish, and fresh dill. Season with salt and pepper. Let the mixture cool.

Roll out the dough on a floured surface until it's about 1/8-inch thick. Use a round cutter or a glass to cut circles from the dough.

Place a spoonful of the fish and dill filling on each dough circle. Fold the dough over the filling to create a half-moon shape, pressing the edges to seal. Crimp the edges with a fork for a decorative touch.

Bring a large pot of salted water to a boil. Cook the pierogi in batches, being careful not to overcrowd the pot. They are done when they float to the surface, about 3 to 4 minutes.

Serve the Fish and Dill Pierogi warm, drizzled with melted butter, and a dollop of sour cream. Garnish with additional chopped dill.

Enjoy your Fish and Dill Pierogi, a delicious and comforting dish that showcases the wonderful combination of seafood and herbs. These pierogi are perfect for a satisfying main course or a special side dish. The flavors of fish and dill wrapped in tender dough create a delightful culinary experience.

Enjoy

66. Lamb and Rosemary Dumplings

Today, we're cooking up Lamb and Rosemary Dumplings, a dish that offers a delightful blend of flavors and textures. The savory taste of lamb, combined with the aromatic rosemary, makes these dumplings a truly special culinary creation. Whether you're looking for a new way to enjoy lamb or just love trying different types of dumplings, this recipe is sure to impress.

Prep: 60 min. Cook: 30 min. Ready in: 1 h. 30 min. Servings: 4

Ingredients:

For the Dumplings:

2 cups all-purpose flour
1/2 teaspoon salt
1/2 cup water
2 tablespoons olive oil

For the Filling:

1 pound ground lamb
1 small onion, finely chopped
2 cloves garlic, minced
1 tablespoon fresh rosemary, finely chopped
1 teaspoon ground cumin
Salt and pepper, to taste

For Cooking:

Vegetable oil, for frying

For the Sauce:

1 cup beef or lamb broth
1 tablespoon tomato paste
1/2 teaspoon sugar
Additional chopped rosemary for garnish

Cooking Directions:

Begin by preparing the dough for the dumplings. In a mixing bowl, combine the flour and salt. Add water and olive oil, mixing until a soft dough forms. Knead the dough on a floured surface until smooth. Let it rest while you prepare the filling.

For the filling, heat a skillet over medium heat. Cook the ground lamb with the onion and garlic until the lamb is browned and the onions are translucent. Drain any excess fat. Stir in the chopped rosemary, ground cumin, salt, and pepper. Cook for a few more minutes, then remove from heat and let cool.

Roll out the dough on a floured surface. Cut it into small circles using a cookie cutter or a glass.

Spoon a small amount of the lamb filling onto each dough circle. Fold the dough over the filling to form a half-moon shape, pressing the edges to seal them tightly.

Heat vegetable oil in a frying pan. Fry the dumplings in batches until golden brown on both sides.

For the sauce, in a saucepan, combine the broth, tomato paste, and sugar. Bring to a simmer, stirring until the sauce thickens slightly.

Serve the Lamb and Rosemary Dumplings with the sauce, garnished with additional rosemary.

Enjoy your Lamb and Rosemary Dumplings, a dish that's sure to be a hit with its rich flavors and comforting warmth. Whether served as a main dish or a unique appetizer, these dumplings offer a delightful way to experience the classic combination of lamb and rosemary in a new and exciting form.

<u>Enjoy</u>

67. Beef Bourguignon Dumplings

Today, we're bringing a gourmet twist to traditional dumplings with Beef Bourguignon Dumplings. This dish is a beautiful combination of a beloved French classic and the universally loved dumpling, offering a unique and memorable culinary experience.

Prep: 1 h. 30 min. Cook: 2 h (for Beef Bourguignon) + 20 min. (for dumplings) Ready in: 3 h. 50 min. Servings: 4

Ingredients:

For the Beef Bourguignon Filling:

1 pound beef chuck, cut into small cubes
2 tablespoons olive oil
1 small onion, finely chopped
1 carrot, finely chopped
2 cloves garlic, minced
1 cup red wine
2 cups beef broth
1 tablespoon tomato paste
1 teaspoon fresh thyme
1 bay leaf
Salt and pepper, to taste
1/2 cup pearl onions, cooked
1/2 cup mushrooms, sautéed

For the Dumpling Dough:

2 cups all-purpose flour
1/2 teaspoon salt
1/2 cup water
2 tablespoons vegetable oil

Cooking Directions:

Start with the Beef Bourguignon filling. In a large pot or Dutch oven, heat the olive oil over medium-high heat. Brown the beef cubes on all sides and set them aside.

In the same pot, add the onion and carrot, cooking until softened. Add the garlic and cook for another minute.

Return the beef to the pot. Stir in the red wine, scraping any browned bits from the bottom of the pot. Add the beef broth, tomato paste, thyme, and bay leaf. Season with salt and pepper.

Bring to a boil, then reduce heat to low and simmer, covered, for about 1.5 to 2 hours, or until the beef is tender. Add the cooked pearl onions and mushrooms in the last 30 minutes of cooking. Let the mixture cool, and then finely chop the beef to create a filling.

Prepare the dumpling dough by mixing the flour and salt in a bowl. Add the water and vegetable oil, mixing to form a smooth dough. Knead briefly, then let it rest for about 30 minutes.

Roll out the dough on a floured surface and cut it into small circles.

Place a spoonful of the Beef Bourguignon filling on each dough circle. Fold the dough over the filling to create a half-moon shape, pressing the edges to seal.

Cook the dumplings in boiling water for about 10 minutes, or until they float to the surface.

Serve the Beef Bourguignon Dumplings hot, perhaps with a side of the remaining stew sauce or a simple gravy.

Savor the rich and savory flavors of Beef Bourguignon Dumplings, a dish that brings a touch of gourmet elegance to the humble dumpling. This recipe is perfect for a special occasion or when you want to impress with a dish that's both comforting and sophisticated.

Enjoy

68. Turkey & Sage Dumplings

Today, we're making Turkey & Sage Dumplings, a delightful dish that brings together the classic flavors of turkey and sage in a comforting package. This recipe is ideal for those who appreciate the simple pleasures of home-cooked meals and are looking for a creative way to use leftover turkey.

Prep: 45 min. Cook: 20 min. Ready in: 1 h. 5 min. Servings: 4

Ingredients:

For the Dumplings:

2 cups all-purpose flour

1/2 teaspoon salt

1/2 cup water

2 tablespoons unsalted butter, melted

For the Filling:

1 cup cooked turkey, finely chopped

1/4 cup celery, finely chopped

1/4 cup onion, finely chopped

2 tablespoons fresh sage, chopped

Salt and pepper, to taste

1/4 cup chicken or turkey broth

For Cooking:

Vegetable oil, for frying

Cooking Directions:

Begin by preparing the dumpling dough. In a large mixing bowl, combine the flour and salt. Add the melted butter and gradually pour in the water, stirring until a smooth dough forms. Knead the dough on a floured surface until it's soft and elastic. Let it rest for about 30 minutes.

For the filling, mix together the chopped turkey, celery, onion, and sage in a bowl. Season with salt and pepper. Add enough broth to moisten the mixture, but ensure it's not too wet.

Roll out the dough on a floured surface. Cut it into small circles using a cookie cutter or a glass.

Place a spoonful of the turkey filling onto each dough circle. Fold the dough over the filling to form a half-moon shape and press the edges to seal them tightly.

Heat vegetable oil in a frying pan over medium heat. Fry the dumplings in batches until they are golden brown on both sides. Drain them on paper towels to remove excess oil.

Serve the Turkey & Sage Dumplings hot. They are delightful on their own or paired with gravy or a light sauce.

Enjoy your Turkey & Sage Dumplings, a cozy and heartwarming dish that's perfect for a family meal or a comforting dinner. These dumplings are a great way to savor the flavors of turkey and sage in a new and exciting form. Share and delight in this homely and delicious creation.

Enjoy

69. Duck and Hoisin Dumplings

Indulge in the rich and aromatic flavors of Duck and Hoisin Dumplings, a dish that seamlessly blends the elegance of duck with the classic Asian condiment, hoisin sauce. These dumplings are a fantastic choice for a special appetizer or a flavorful snack.

Prep: 60 min. Cook: 20 min. Ready in: 1 h. 20 min. Servings: 4

Ingredients:

For the Dumplings:
Store-bought or homemade dumpling wrappers

For the Filling:
1 cup cooked duck meat, finely chopped
1/4 cup hoisin sauce
2 green onions, finely chopped
1 teaspoon sesame oil
1 teaspoon grated ginger
1 clove garlic, minced
Salt and pepper, to taste

For Cooking:
Vegetable oil, for frying
Water, for steaming

For the Dipping Sauce:
1/4 cup soy sauce
1 tablespoon rice vinegar
1 teaspoon sesame oil
1/2 teaspoon honey
1/2 teaspoon grated ginger
1 clove garlic, minced

Cooking Directions:

Begin by preparing the filling. In a bowl, mix together the chopped duck meat, hoisin sauce, green onions, sesame oil, grated ginger, and minced garlic. Season with salt and pepper. The mixture should be flavorful and cohesive.

Lay out the dumpling wrappers on a clean surface. Place a small spoonful of the duck and hoisin filling in the center of each wrapper.

Moisten the edges of the wrapper with water, fold it over the filling, and press to seal, forming a half-moon shape. Ensure the edges are tightly sealed.

To cook the dumplings, you can either pan-fry or steam them. For pan-frying, heat some oil in a skillet and fry the dumplings until golden brown on both sides. For steaming, place the dumplings in a steamer lined with parchment paper and steam for about 10 minutes.

While the dumplings are cooking, prepare the dipping sauce. In a small bowl, mix together soy sauce, rice vinegar, sesame oil, honey, grated ginger, and minced garlic.

Serve the Duck and Hoisin Dumplings hot, with the dipping sauce on the side. Each dumpling should offer a burst of the rich and savory flavors of duck, complemented by the sweet and tangy hoisin sauce.

Savor the exquisite taste of Duck and Hoisin Dumplings, a dish that's sure to impress with its depth of flavor and elegant presentation. Whether you're hosting a dinner party or enjoying a quiet evening at home, these dumplings provide a delicious and satisfying culinary experience.

Enjoy

70. Bacon, Egg, and Cheese Bao

Today, we're creating Bacon, Egg, and Cheese Bao, a dish that brings a delightful twist to your breakfast routine. This recipe combines the comforting flavors of a classic American breakfast with the soft, pillowy texture of Chinese bao buns, making it a fun and tasty fusion dish.

Prep: 2 h. (including dough rising time) Cook: 20 min. Ready in: 2 h. 20 min. Servings: 4

Ingredients:

For the Bao Dough:

2 cups all-purpose flour

1 tablespoon sugar

1/2 teaspoon salt

1 teaspoon instant yeast

2/3 cup warm water

1 tablespoon vegetable oil

For the Filling:

4 strips bacon, cooked and chopped

4 eggs, scrambled

1/2 cup shredded cheddar cheese

Salt and pepper, to taste

Cooking Directions:

Begin by preparing the bao dough. In a large mixing bowl, combine the flour, sugar, salt, and instant yeast. Add the warm water and vegetable oil, mixing to form a soft dough. Knead the dough on a floured surface until smooth and elastic, about 10 minutes. Place the dough in a greased bowl, cover, and let it rise in a warm place for about 1 to 1.5 hours, or until doubled in size.

While the dough is rising, prepare the filling. In a pan, cook the bacon until crispy, then chop it into small pieces. Scramble the eggs and season with salt and pepper. Mix the bacon, scrambled eggs, and shredded cheddar cheese in a bowl.

Punch down the risen dough and divide it into 8 equal pieces. Roll each piece into a ball, then flatten each ball into a disc. Place a spoonful of the bacon, egg, and cheese mixture in the center of each disc.

Gather the edges of the dough around the filling, pinching them together at the top to seal. Let the filled bao buns rest for about 15-20 minutes.

Steam the bao buns in a steamer for about 10-12 minutes, or until they are puffed and cooked through.

Serve the Bacon, Egg, and Cheese Bao warm. They are perfect as a standalone breakfast treat or paired with your favorite morning beverage.

Enjoy your Bacon, Egg, and Cheese Bao, a fusion dish that's sure to start your day off right. These bao buns offer a fun and flavorful twist on the traditional breakfast, combining familiar tastes in a novel and delightful way. Perfect for a weekend brunch or a special breakfast occasion!

Enjoy

71. Sausage and Maple Syrup Dumplings

Today, we're making Sausage and Maple Syrup Dumplings, a delightful dish that combines the comforting flavors of a hearty breakfast in a fun and enjoyable format. These dumplings are perfect for those who love a sweet and savory combination and are looking for something different in their culinary adventures.

Prep: 45 min. Cook: 20 min. Ready in: 1 h. 5 min. Servings: 4

Ingredients:

For the Dumplings:

2 cups all-purpose flour

1/2 teaspoon salt

1/2 cup water

2 tablespoons unsalted butter, melted

For the Filling:

1/2 pound breakfast sausage, cooked and crumbled

2 tablespoons maple syrup

1/4 cup onion, finely chopped

1/4 cup cheddar cheese, grated

Salt and pepper, to taste

For Cooking:

Vegetable oil, for frying

For Serving:

Additional maple syrup for drizzling

Cooking Directions:

Begin by preparing the dumpling dough. In a large mixing bowl, combine the flour and salt. Add the melted butter and gradually pour in the water, stirring until a smooth dough forms. Knead the dough on a floured surface until it's soft and elastic. Let it rest for about 30 minutes.

For the filling, mix together the cooked and crumbled breakfast sausage, maple syrup, onion, and cheddar cheese. Season with salt and pepper. The mixture should be flavorful and cohesive.

Roll out the dough on a floured surface. Cut it into small circles using a cookie cutter or a glass.

Place a spoonful of the sausage and maple syrup filling onto each dough circle. Fold the dough over the filling to form a half-moon shape, pressing the edges to seal them tightly.

Heat vegetable oil in a frying pan over medium heat. Fry the dumplings in batches until they are golden brown on both sides. Drain them on paper towels to remove excess oil.

Serve the Sausage and Maple Syrup Dumplings warm, drizzled with additional maple syrup for extra sweetness.

Enjoy your Sausage and Maple Syrup Dumplings, a dish that's sure to be a hit with its unique blend of flavors. These dumplings are perfect for a brunch, a special breakfast, or as a delightful snack. The combination of savory sausage and sweet maple syrup wrapped in a tender dough makes for a truly comforting and satisfying experience.

Enjoy

72. Blueberry Pancake Dumplings

Today, we're making Blueberry Pancake Dumplings, a playful and delicious dish that brings a new twist to a breakfast favorite. These dumplings are a delightful way to enjoy the flavors of blueberry pancakes in a fun, bite-sized form, perfect for a special breakfast or brunch.

Prep: 30 min. Cook: 15 min. Ready in: 45 min. Servings: 4

Ingredients:

For the Pancake Batter:

1 1/2 cups all-purpose flour
2 tablespoons sugar
1/2 teaspoon baking powder
1/2 teaspoon baking soda
A pinch of salt
1 cup buttermilk
1 egg
2 tablespoons unsalted butter, melted

For the Filling:

1 cup blueberries (fresh or frozen)
1 tablespoon sugar
1 teaspoon lemon zest

For Cooking:

Additional butter, for frying

For Serving:

Maple syrup
Powdered sugar
Additional blueberries

Cooking Directions:

Start by preparing the pancake batter. In a large bowl, whisk together the flour, sugar, baking powder, baking soda, and a pinch of salt. In another bowl, mix the buttermilk, egg, and melted butter. Add the wet ingredients to the dry ingredients and stir until just combined.

For the filling, toss the blueberries with sugar and lemon zest.

Heat a non-stick skillet over medium heat and melt a small amount of butter.

Drop spoonfuls of the pancake batter onto the skillet to form small pancakes. Place a few sugared blueberries on top of each pancake. Spoon a little more batter over the blueberries to encase them in the pancake.

Cook the pancakes for about 2 minutes on each side, or until they are golden brown and the batter is cooked through.

Serve the Blueberry Pancake Dumplings warm, drizzled with maple syrup and sprinkled with powdered sugar. Add a few fresh blueberries on the side for garnish.

Enjoy your Blueberry Pancake Dumplings, a delightful dish that's sure to bring a smile to everyone at the table. These dumplings are a great way to start your day with the sweet taste of blueberries and the comforting feel of pancakes, all in one delightful package. Perfect for a weekend brunch or a special breakfast treat!

Enjoy

73. Cinnamon Roll Dumplings

Today, we're making Cinnamon Roll Dumplings, a delightful treat that combines the sweet, spicy essence of cinnamon rolls with the fun and versatility of dumplings. This recipe is a perfect choice for a sweet breakfast, a dessert, or a special snack to enjoy with your afternoon coffee or tea.

Prep: 60 min. Cook: 20 min. Ready in: 1 h. 20 min. Servings: 4

Ingredients:

For the Dough:
2 cups all-purpose flour
1/4 cup sugar
1/2 teaspoon salt
1 teaspoon instant yeast
3/4 cup warm milk
2 tablespoons unsalted butter, melted

For the Filling:
1/4 cup unsalted butter, softened
1/2 cup brown sugar
2 tablespoons ground cinnamon

For the Glaze:
1 cup powdered sugar
2 tablespoons milk
1/2 teaspoon vanilla extract

Cooking Directions:

Begin by preparing the dough. In a mixing bowl, combine the flour, sugar, salt, and instant yeast. Add the warm milk and melted butter, and mix until a soft dough forms. Knead the dough on a floured surface until smooth and elastic. Place the dough in a greased bowl, cover, and let it rise in a warm place for about 45 minutes, or until doubled in size.
For the filling, mix together the softened butter, brown sugar, and ground cinnamon in a bowl.
Once the dough has risen, roll it out on a floured surface into a rectangle about 1/4 inch thick. Spread the cinnamon filling evenly over the dough.
Roll the dough up tightly from the long side, then slice it into 1-inch thick pieces.
Prepare a steamer with parchment paper. Place the sliced dough pieces, cut side up, in the steamer, making sure they are not touching as they will expand.
Steam the dumplings for about 15-20 minutes, or until they are puffed up and cooked through.
While the dumplings are steaming, prepare the glaze. In a small bowl, whisk together the powdered sugar, milk, and vanilla extract until smooth.
Once the dumplings are done, let them cool slightly, then drizzle with the glaze.

Enjoy your Cinnamon Roll Dumplings, a sweet and satisfying twist on the classic cinnamon roll. These dumplings are perfect for indulging your sweet tooth and are sure to be a hit with anyone who loves the comforting flavor of cinnamon. Serve them warm for a truly delightful experience.

Enjoy

74. Pizza Dumplings

Today, we're creating Pizza Dumplings, a dish that's sure to excite both pizza enthusiasts and dumpling lovers alike. This unique fusion recipe encapsulates the beloved flavors of pizza in a fun and easy-to-eat dumpling format, making it a great choice for parties, snacks, or a family-friendly meal.

Prep: 45 min. Cook: 20 min. Ready in: 1 h. 5 min. Servings: 4

Ingredients:

For the Dumpling Dough:

2 cups all-purpose flour
1/2 teaspoon salt
1/2 cup water
2 tablespoons olive oil

For the Pizza Filling:

1/2 cup marinara sauce
1 cup mozzarella cheese, shredded
1/2 cup pepperoni, chopped
1/4 cup bell peppers, finely chopped
1/4 cup onions, finely chopped
1 teaspoon Italian seasoning
Salt and pepper, to taste

For Cooking:

Vegetable oil, for frying

Cooking Directions:

Begin by preparing the dumpling dough. In a large mixing bowl, combine the flour and salt. Add the water and olive oil, mixing to form a smooth dough. Knead the dough on a floured surface until it's soft and elastic. Let it rest for about 30 minutes.

For the pizza filling, in a bowl, mix together the marinara sauce, mozzarella cheese, pepperoni, bell peppers, onions, and Italian seasoning. Season with salt and pepper.

Roll out the dough on a floured surface. Cut it into small circles using a cookie cutter or a glass.

Place a spoonful of the pizza filling onto each dough circle. Fold the dough over the filling to form a half-moon shape, pressing the edges to seal them tightly.

Heat vegetable oil in a frying pan over medium heat. Fry the dumplings in batches until they are golden brown on both sides. Drain them on paper towels to remove excess oil.

Serve the Pizza Dumplings hot, with additional marinara sauce for dipping. These dumplings should offer the comforting taste of pizza with the enjoyable texture of a crispy dumpling.

Savor the delightful flavors of Pizza Dumplings, a fusion dish that brings a twist to traditional favorites. Whether you're hosting a gathering or just enjoying a casual meal, these dumplings offer a fun and delicious way to enjoy the classic taste of pizza in a new and exciting form.

Enjoy

75. Tandoori Chicken Bao

Today, we're making Tandoori Chicken Bao, a creative fusion dish that combines the bold and vibrant flavors of Indian cuisine with the delicate, pillowy texture of Chinese bao buns. This recipe is a delightful way to explore different culinary traditions and enjoy a fusion of tastes.

Prep: 2 h. Cook: 30 min. Ready in: 2 h. 30 min. Servings: 4

Ingredients:

For the Tandoori Chicken:

1 pound chicken breast, cut into small pieces

1/2 cup plain yogurt

2 tablespoons tandoori masala

1 teaspoon garlic paste

1 teaspoon ginger paste

Juice of 1 lemon

Salt to taste

For the Bao Dough:

2 cups all-purpose flour

1 tablespoon sugar

1/2 teaspoon salt

1 teaspoon instant yeast

2/3 cup warm water

1 tablespoon vegetable oil

For Serving:

Fresh cilantro, chopped

Yogurt or mint chutney (optional)

Cooking Directions:

Begin by marinating the chicken for the tandoori filling. In a bowl, mix together the yogurt, tandoori masala, garlic paste, ginger paste, lemon juice, and salt. Add the chicken pieces and ensure they're well-coated with the marinade. Let it marinate in the refrigerator for at least 1 hour.
Prepare the bao dough. In a large mixing bowl, combine the flour, sugar, salt, and instant yeast. Add the warm water and vegetable oil, mixing to form a soft dough. Knead the dough on a floured surface until smooth and elastic. Place the dough in a greased bowl, cover, and let it rise in a warm place for about 1 hour, or until doubled in size.
While the dough is rising, cook the tandoori chicken. Preheat the oven to 400°F (200°C). Place the marinated chicken on a baking sheet lined with aluminum foil. Bake for 20-25 minutes, or until the chicken is cooked through.
Once the dough has risen, punch it down and divide it into small equal-sized balls. Roll each ball into a flat circle, then place a spoonful of the cooked tandoori chicken in the center.
Gather the edges of the dough circle around the filling, pinching them together at the top to seal. Let the filled bao buns rest for about 15-20 minutes.
Steam the bao buns in a steamer for about 10-12 minutes, or until they are puffed and cooked through.
Serve the Tandoori Chicken Bao warm, garnished with chopped cilantro. You can also serve them with yogurt or mint chutney on the side for added flavor.

Enjoy your Tandoori Chicken Bao, a dish that's as enjoyable to eat as it is to prepare. This fusion of Indian and Chinese cuisines offers a unique and flavorful experience, perfect for a special meal or when you want to impress with your culinary skills. The combination of spicy tandoori chicken and soft bao buns is sure to delight your taste buds.

Enjoy

76. Taco Empanada Dumplings

Today, we're making Taco Empanada Dumplings, a dish that's sure to excite with its blend of bold taco flavors and the comforting texture of empanadas. This fusion recipe is ideal for a fun and flavorful meal, snack, or as a part of a festive spread.

Prep: 45 min. Cook: 20 min. Ready in: 1 h. 5 min. Servings: 4

Ingredients:

For the Empanada Dough:

2 cups all-purpose flour

1/2 teaspoon salt

1/3 cup vegetable oil

1/2 cup warm water

For the Taco Filling:

1 tablespoon vegetable oil

1/2 pound ground beef

1 small onion, finely chopped

2 cloves garlic, minced

1 tablespoon taco seasoning

1/2 cup tomato sauce

1/2 cup black beans, drained and rinsed

Salt and pepper, to taste

1/2 cup cheddar cheese, shredded

For Cooking:

Vegetable oil, for frying

For Serving:

Sour cream

Salsa

Fresh cilantro, chopped

Cooking Directions:

Begin by preparing the empanada dough. In a large mixing bowl, combine the flour and salt. Add the vegetable oil and warm water, mixing to form a soft dough. Knead the dough on a floured surface until smooth and elastic. Let it rest for about 30 minutes.

For the taco filling, heat oil in a pan over medium heat. Cook the ground beef with the onion and garlic until the beef is browned. Drain any excess fat.

Stir in the taco seasoning and tomato sauce. Add the black beans and cook for a few more minutes, until the mixture is well combined and heated through. Season with salt and pepper. Let the filling cool, then mix in the shredded cheddar cheese.

Roll out the empanada dough on a floured surface. Cut it into small circles using a cookie cutter or a glass.

Spoon a small amount of the taco filling onto each dough circle. Fold the dough over the filling to form a half-moon shape, pressing the edges to seal them tightly.

Heat vegetable oil in a frying pan over medium heat. Fry the empanadas in batches until they are golden brown on both sides. Drain them on paper towels to remove excess oil.

Serve the Taco Empanada Dumplings hot, with sour cream, salsa, and chopped cilantro on the side. These dumplings offer a delicious bite of taco flavors wrapped in a crispy, golden pastry.

Enjoy your Taco Empanada Dumplings, a fusion dish that brings a twist to traditional flavors. Perfect for entertaining or as a unique meal option, these dumplings are a crowd-pleaser, combining the best of both Mexican and empanada worlds in every bite.

Enjoy

77. Thai Green Curry Chicken Dumplings

Today, we're making Thai Green Curry Chicken Dumplings, a delightful fusion dish that combines the aromatic flavors of Thai green curry with the satisfying experience of eating dumplings. This recipe is a wonderful way to enjoy a taste of Thailand in a novel and exciting form.

Prep: 60 min. Cook: 20 min. Ready in: 1 h. 20 min. Servings: 4

Ingredients:

For the Dumplings:
Store-bought or homemade dumpling wrappers

For the Filling:
1 tablespoon vegetable oil
1/2 pound chicken breast, finely chopped
2 tablespoons Thai green curry paste
1/2 cup coconut milk
1/4 cup bamboo shoots, finely chopped
1/4 cup carrots, finely chopped

1 tablespoon fish sauce
1 teaspoon sugar
Fresh basil leaves, chopped
Salt, to taste

For Cooking:
Vegetable oil, for frying
Water, for steaming

For the Dipping Sauce:
1/4 cup soy sauce
1 tablespoon lime juice
1 teaspoon honey
1/2 teaspoon chili flakes
1/2 teaspoon grated ginger

Cooking Directions:

Begin by preparing the filling. Heat the vegetable oil in a pan over medium heat. Add the chicken and cook until it's no longer pink. Stir in the green curry paste and cook for a couple of minutes to release the flavors.

Add the coconut milk, bamboo shoots, carrots, fish sauce, and sugar. Cook until the mixture thickens slightly. Stir in the chopped basil and season with salt. Let the mixture cool.

Lay out the dumpling wrappers on a clean surface. Place a small spoonful of the Thai green curry chicken filling in the center of each wrapper.

Moisten the edges of the wrapper with water, fold it over the filling, and press to seal, forming a half-moon shape. Ensure the edges are tightly sealed.

To cook the dumplings, you can either pan-fry or steam them. For pan-frying, heat some oil in a skillet and fry the dumplings until golden brown on both sides. For steaming, place the dumplings in a steamer lined with parchment paper and steam for about 10 minutes.

While the dumplings are cooking, prepare the dipping sauce. In a small bowl, mix together soy sauce, lime juice, honey, chili flakes, and grated ginger.

Serve the Thai Green Curry Chicken Dumplings hot, with the dipping sauce on the side. Each dumpling should offer a burst of the rich and spicy flavors of Thai green curry in a tender and flavorful wrapper.

Enjoy your Thai Green Curry Chicken Dumplings, a fusion dish that's sure to impress with its blend of traditional Thai flavors and the beloved dumpling format. Perfect for a special meal or a creative cooking project, these dumplings bring the best of Thai cuisine to your table in a fun and delicious way.

Enjoy

78. Quinoa and Vegetable Dumplings

Today, we're making Quinoa and Vegetable Dumplings, a delightful dish that offers a healthy and tasty option for dumpling lovers. This recipe combines the nuttiness of quinoa with fresh vegetables, wrapped in a gluten-free dumpling wrapper, making it perfect for those with dietary restrictions or anyone looking for a lighter meal.

Prep: 60 min. Cook: 20 min. Ready in: 1 h. 20 min. Servings: 4

Ingredients:

For the Dumplings:

Gluten-free dumpling wrappers (store-bought or homemade)

For the Filling:

1 cup cooked quinoa
1/2 cup carrots, finely chopped
1/2 cup bell peppers, finely chopped
1/2 cup zucchini, finely chopped
1/4 cup green onions, finely chopped
2 cloves garlic, minced
1 tablespoon soy sauce (gluten-free if needed)
1 teaspoon sesame oil
Salt and pepper, to taste

For Cooking:

Vegetable oil, for frying
Water, for steaming

For the Dipping Sauce:

1/4 cup soy sauce (gluten-free if needed)
1 tablespoon rice vinegar
1 teaspoon honey
1/2 teaspoon grated ginger
1/2 teaspoon sesame oil
Chili flakes (optional)

Cooking Directions:

Begin by preparing the filling. In a large bowl, mix together the cooked quinoa, carrots, bell peppers, zucchini, green onions, and minced garlic. Add the soy sauce, sesame oil, salt, and pepper. Mix well until all the ingredients are evenly combined.

Lay out the gluten-free dumpling wrappers on a clean surface. Place a small amount of the quinoa and vegetable filling in the center of each wrapper.

Moisten the edges of the wrapper with water, fold it over the filling, and press to seal, forming a half-moon shape. Make sure the edges are tightly sealed.

To cook the dumplings, you can either pan-fry or steam them. For pan-frying, heat some oil in a skillet and fry the dumplings until golden brown on both sides. For steaming, place the dumplings in a steamer lined with parchment paper and steam for about 10 minutes.

While the dumplings are cooking, prepare the dipping sauce. In a small bowl, mix together soy sauce, rice vinegar, honey, grated ginger, sesame oil, and chili flakes, if using.

Serve the Quinoa and Vegetable Dumplings hot, with the dipping sauce on the side. These dumplings are a delightful blend of wholesome ingredients, offering a satisfying and guilt-free dining experience.

Enjoy your Quinoa and Vegetable Dumplings, a dish that's as nutritious as it is delicious. Whether you're catering to gluten-free needs or simply seeking a healthier alternative, these dumplings provide a wonderful combination of flavors and textures, making them a great addition to any meal.

Enjoy

79. Gluten-Free Prawn Har Gow

Today, we're making Gluten-Free Prawn Har Gow, a dish that brings the exquisite flavors of traditional Chinese cuisine to those following a gluten-free diet. These dumplings are known for their translucent, tender wrappers and succulent prawn filling, making them a favorite at dim sum restaurants.

Prep: 60 min. Cook: 105 min. Ready in: 1 h. 10 min. Servings: 4

Ingredients:

For the Dough:
1 cup gluten-free wheat starch
1/2 cup tapioca starch
1 cup boiling water
1 tablespoon vegetable oil

For the Filling:
1/2 pound prawns, peeled, deveined, and finely chopped
1 tablespoon bamboo shoots, finely chopped (optional)
1 green onion, finely chopped
1 teaspoon ginger, grated
1 tablespoon gluten-free soy sauce
1 teaspoon sesame oil
Salt and pepper, to taste

Cooking Directions:

Begin by preparing the dough. In a mixing bowl, combine the gluten-free wheat starch and tapioca starch. Gradually pour in the boiling water while stirring. Add the vegetable oil and mix until a dough forms. Knead the dough until it becomes smooth and pliable. Cover and set aside.

For the filling, combine the chopped prawns, bamboo shoots (if using), green onion, ginger, gluten-free soy sauce, sesame oil, salt, and pepper in a bowl. Mix well until the ingredients are evenly distributed.

Divide the dough into small portions. Roll each portion into a ball, then flatten it into a small circle about 3 inches in diameter. The dough should be thin but not too fragile.

Place a spoonful of the prawn filling in the center of each dough circle. Carefully fold the dough over the filling and pleat the edges to seal, forming a crescent shape.

Prepare a steamer by lining it with parchment paper. Arrange the Har Gow in the steamer, ensuring they are not touching as they will expand during cooking.

Steam the Har Gow for about 10 minutes, or until the wrappers become translucent and the filling is cooked through.

Serve the Gluten-Free Prawn Har Gow hot, accompanied by a dipping sauce of your choice, such as a simple mixture of gluten-free soy sauce and chili oil.

Enjoy your Gluten-Free Prawn Har Gow, a dish that beautifully captures the essence of traditional dim sum while catering to gluten-free dietary needs. These dumplings are perfect for sharing and are sure to delight with their delicate wrappers and flavorful filling.

Enjoy

80. Gluten-Free Chicken & Herb Dumplings

Today, we're making Gluten-Free Chicken & Herb Dumplings, a dish that brings the comforting flavors of a classic meal to those with gluten sensitivities. These dumplings combine the savory taste of chicken with the freshness of herbs, all wrapped in a delicate gluten-free dough.

Prep: 60 min. Cook: 20 min. Ready in: 1 h. 20 min. Servings: 4

Ingredients:

For the Dumpling Dough:

1 1/2 cups gluten-free all-purpose flour
1/2 teaspoon xanthan gum (if not included in the flour blend)
1/2 teaspoon salt
1/2 cup water
2 tablespoons olive oil

For the Filling:

1 cup cooked chicken, finely chopped
1/4 cup carrots, finely chopped
1/4 cup celery, finely chopped
1 tablespoon fresh parsley, chopped
1 teaspoon fresh thyme, chopped
Salt and pepper, to taste
1 tablespoon gluten-free chicken broth

Cooking Directions:

Begin by preparing the dough. In a large mixing bowl, combine the gluten-free flour, xanthan gum (if using), and salt. Gradually add the water and olive oil, mixing until a smooth dough forms. Knead the dough briefly until it becomes pliable. Cover and set aside to rest.

For the filling, mix together the chopped chicken, carrots, celery, parsley, thyme, salt, pepper, and chicken broth in a bowl. The mixture should be moist but not too wet.

Divide the dough into small portions. Roll each portion into a ball, then flatten it into a small circle.

Place a spoonful of the chicken and herb filling in the center of each dough circle. Fold the dough over the filling to create a half-moon shape, pressing the edges to seal them tightly.

Bring a large pot of salted water to a gentle boil. Carefully add the dumplings to the boiling water and cook for about 10 minutes, or until they float to the surface and the dough is cooked through.

Serve the Gluten-Free Chicken & Herb Dumplings hot. They can be enjoyed on their own or with a side of gluten-free gravy or sauce for added flavor.

Savor the delightful taste of Gluten-Free Chicken & Herb Dumplings, a dish that's both nourishing and satisfying. These dumplings are a great option for a cozy family dinner, offering a gluten-free alternative that doesn't compromise on taste or texture.

Enjoy

81. Dairy-Free Spinach and Pine Nut Dumplings

Today, we're making Dairy-Free Spinach and Pine Nut Dumplings, a dish that's not only healthy and nutritious but also packed with flavor. This recipe is perfect for those who love the combination of earthy spinach and nutty pine nuts, all wrapped up in a tender dumpling.

Prep: 45 min. Cook: 20 min. Ready in: 1 h. 5 min. Servings: 4

Ingredients:

For the Dumplings:

2 cups all-purpose flour

1/2 teaspoon salt

1/2 cup water

2 tablespoons olive oil

For the Filling:

2 cups spinach, chopped

1/4 cup pine nuts, toasted

2 cloves garlic, minced

1 small onion, finely chopped

2 tablespoons olive oil

Salt and pepper, to taste

A pinch of nutmeg

For Cooking:

Additional olive oil or vegetable oil, for frying

Cooking Directions:

Begin by preparing the dumpling dough. In a large mixing bowl, combine the flour and salt. Gradually add the water and olive oil, mixing to form a smooth dough. Knead the dough on a floured surface until it's soft and elastic. Let it rest for about 30 minutes.

For the filling, heat the olive oil in a pan over medium heat. Sauté the onion and garlic until the onion is translucent. Add the spinach and cook until it wilts. Stir in the toasted pine nuts, salt, pepper, and a pinch of nutmeg. Let the mixture cool.

Roll out the dough on a floured surface. Cut it into small circles using a cookie cutter or a glass.

Place a spoonful of the spinach and pine nut filling onto each dough circle. Fold the dough over the filling to form a half-moon shape, pressing the edges to seal them tightly.

Heat additional olive oil or vegetable oil in a frying pan over medium heat. Fry the dumplings in batches until they are golden brown on both sides. Drain them on paper towels to remove excess oil.

Serve the Dairy-Free Spinach and Pine Nut Dumplings hot. They are delightful on their own or paired with a dipping sauce of your choice, such as a tangy vinaigrette or a simple tomato sauce.

Enjoy your Dairy-Free Spinach and Pine Nut Dumplings, a dish that's as delicious as it is nutritious. Whether you're catering to dietary restrictions or simply seeking a healthy, flavorful meal, these dumplings are sure to satisfy with their combination of fresh spinach and rich pine nuts.

Enjoy

82. Dairy-Free Shrimp & Cilantro Dumplings

Today, we're making Dairy-Free Shrimp & Cilantro Dumplings, a dish that's both healthy and bursting with flavor. This recipe is perfect for those who love the combination of tender shrimp and the vibrant taste of cilantro, all encased in a delicate dumpling.

Prep: 60 min. Cook: 20 min. Ready in: 1 h. 20 min. Servings: 4

Ingredients:

For the Dumplings:

Dairy-free dumpling wrappers (store-bought or homemade)

For the Filling:

1 pound shrimp, peeled, deveined, and finely chopped

1/4 cup cilantro, finely chopped

1 green onion, finely chopped

1 teaspoon grated ginger

1 clove garlic, minced

1 tablespoon soy sauce (ensure it's dairy-free)

1 teaspoon sesame oil

Salt and pepper, to taste

For Cooking:

Vegetable oil, for frying

Water, for steaming

For the Dipping Sauce:

1/4 cup soy sauce

1 tablespoon rice vinegar

1 teaspoon sesame oil

1/2 teaspoon sugar

1/2 teaspoon grated ginger

1 clove garlic, minced

Chili flakes (optional)

Cooking Directions:

Begin by preparing the filling. In a large bowl, combine the finely chopped shrimp, cilantro, green onion, grated ginger, minced garlic, soy sauce, and sesame oil. Season with salt and pepper. Mix well until the ingredients are evenly combined and the mixture is cohesive.

Lay out the dairy-free dumpling wrappers on a clean surface. Place a small amount of the shrimp and cilantro filling in the center of each wrapper.

Moisten the edges of the wrapper with water, fold it over the filling, and press to seal, forming a half-moon shape. Ensure the edges are tightly sealed.

To cook the dumplings, you can either pan-fry or steam them. For pan-frying, heat some oil in a skillet and fry the dumplings until golden brown on both sides. For steaming, place the dumplings in a steamer lined with parchment paper and steam for about 10 minutes.

While the dumplings are cooking, prepare the dipping sauce. In a small bowl, mix together soy sauce, rice vinegar, sesame oil, sugar, grated ginger, minced garlic, and chili flakes, if using.

Serve the Dairy-Free Shrimp & Cilantro Dumplings hot, with the dipping sauce on the side. Each dumpling should offer a burst of the rich and savory flavors of shrimp, complemented by the fresh cilantro and the tangy dipping sauce.

Enjoy your Dairy-Free Shrimp & Cilantro Dumplings, a dish that's sure to delight with its blend of fresh ingredients and rich flavors. Perfect for a light meal, an appetizer, or a special occasion, these dumplings offer a delicious and health-conscious option for enjoying the timeless taste of shrimp dumplings.

Enjoy

83. Spicy Beef & Szechuan Pepper Dumplings

Today, we're making Spicy Beef & Szechuan Pepper Dumplings, a dish that's sure to awaken your taste buds. The unique combination of spicy beef and numbing Szechuan pepper creates a flavor profile that is both exciting and addictive, making these dumplings a must-try for lovers of spicy food.

Prep: 60 min. Cook: 20 min. Ready in: 1 h. 20 min. Servings: 4

Ingredients:

For the Dumplings:
Store-bought or homemade dumpling wrappers

For the Filling:
1 pound ground beef
1 tablespoon Szechuan peppercorns, ground
1 tablespoon soy sauce
2 teaspoons chili oil
1 teaspoon Chinese five-spice powder
2 green onions, finely chopped
1 tablespoon ginger, grated
2 cloves garlic, minced

Salt to taste

For Cooking:
Vegetable oil, for frying
Water, for steaming

For the Dipping Sauce:
1/4 cup soy sauce
1 tablespoon rice vinegar
1 teaspoon sesame oil
1/2 teaspoon sugar
1 clove garlic, minced
1/2 teaspoon grated ginger
Chili flakes (optional)

Cooking Directions:

Begin by preparing the filling. In a large bowl, mix together the ground beef, ground Szechuan peppercorns, soy sauce, chili oil, Chinese five-spice powder, green onions, grated ginger, and minced garlic. Season with salt and mix well until all ingredients are thoroughly combined.

Lay out the dumpling wrappers on a clean surface. Place a small amount of the spicy beef filling in the center of each wrapper.

Moisten the edges of the wrapper with water, fold it over the filling, and press to seal, forming a half-moon shape. Ensure the edges are tightly sealed.

To cook the dumplings, you can either pan-fry or steam them. For pan-frying, heat some oil in a skillet and fry the dumplings until golden brown on both sides. For steaming, place the dumplings in a steamer lined with parchment paper and steam for about 10 minutes.

While the dumplings are cooking, prepare the dipping sauce. In a small bowl, mix together soy sauce, rice vinegar, sesame oil, sugar, minced garlic, grated ginger, and chili flakes, if using.

Serve the Spicy Beef & Szechuan Pepper Dumplings hot, with the dipping sauce on the side. Each dumpling should offer a rich and complex flavor with a satisfying balance of heat and numbing sensations.

Enjoy your Spicy Beef & Szechuan Pepper Dumplings, a dish that's as bold in flavor as it is in character. Perfect for a spicy food challenge, a flavorful dinner, or as a standout dish at your next gathering, these dumplings are sure to be a conversation starter and a palate pleaser.

Enjoy

84. Spicy Tofu & Kimchi Dumplings

Today, we're making Spicy Tofu & Kimchi Dumplings, a vegan dish that packs a punch with its vibrant flavors. The combination of spicy kimchi and hearty tofu makes these dumplings a delicious and satisfying option for anyone who loves the depth and heat of Korean flavors.

Prep: 45 min. Cook: 20 min. Ready in: 1 h. 5 min. Servings: 4

Ingredients:

For the Dumplings:
Store-bought or homemade dumpling wrappers

For the Filling:
1 cup firm tofu, crumbled
1 cup kimchi, finely chopped
1 tablespoon sesame oil
1 green onion, finely chopped
1 clove garlic, minced
1 teaspoon grated ginger
1 tablespoon soy sauce
1 teaspoon gochugaru (Korean red pepper flakes) or to taste
Salt to taste

For Cooking:
Vegetable oil, for frying
Water, for steaming

For the Dipping Sauce:
1/4 cup soy sauce
1 tablespoon rice vinegar
1 teaspoon sesame oil
1/2 teaspoon sugar
1 clove garlic, minced
1/2 teaspoon grated ginger
Optional: chili flakes for extra heat

Cooking Directions:

Begin by preparing the filling. In a bowl, combine the crumbled tofu, finely chopped kimchi, sesame oil, green onion, minced garlic, grated ginger, soy sauce, and gochugaru. Season with salt and mix well until all ingredients are thoroughly combined.

Lay out the dumpling wrappers on a clean surface. Place a small amount of the tofu and kimchi filling in the center of each wrapper.

Moisten the edges of the wrapper with water, fold it over the filling, and press to seal, forming a half-moon shape. Ensure the edges are tightly sealed.

To cook the dumplings, you can either pan-fry or steam them. For pan-frying, heat some oil in a skillet and fry the dumplings until golden brown on both sides. For steaming, place the dumplings in a steamer lined with parchment paper and steam for about 10 minutes.

While the dumplings are cooking, prepare the dipping sauce. In a small bowl, mix together soy sauce, rice vinegar, sesame oil, sugar, minced garlic, grated ginger, and chili flakes, if using.

Serve the Spicy Tofu & Kimchi Dumplings hot, with the dipping sauce on the side. Each dumpling should offer a flavorful burst of spicy and tangy kimchi, balanced with the subtle, savory notes of tofu.

Enjoy your Spicy Tofu & Kimchi Dumplings, a dish that brings the essence of Korean flavors to your table in a fun and delicious way. Perfect for a flavorful snack, an appetizer, or part of a larger meal, these dumplings are sure to delight lovers of spicy and bold tastes.

Enjoy

85. Xiao Long Bao (Pork Soup Dumplings)

Today, we're making Xiao Long Bao, also known as Pork Soup Dumplings. These dumplings are a marvel of Chinese cuisine, combining a rich, savory filling with a delightful burst of hot soup, all encased in a tender, thin wrapper. The process of making Xiao Long Bao is both intricate and rewarding.

Prep: 2 h. Cook: 20 min. Ready in: 2 h. 20 min. Servings: 4

Ingredients:

For the Dough:

2 cups all-purpose flour
3/4 cup warm water

For the Soup Gelatin:

2 cups chicken broth
1/2 cup pork skin or chicken feet (for natural gelatin)
1 slice ginger

For the Filling:

1/2 pound ground pork
1 teaspoon soy sauce
1 teaspoon Shaoxing wine (or dry sherry)
1/2 teaspoon sesame oil
1/2 teaspoon sugar
1/4 teaspoon white pepper
1/4 cup finely chopped green onions
1 tablespoon grated ginger

For Cooking:

Cabbage leaves or parchment paper for steaming

Cooking Directions:

Start by making the soup gelatin. Combine the chicken broth, pork skin or chicken feet, and ginger in a pot. Simmer for about 1 hour, then strain. Pour the broth into a shallow dish and refrigerate until set into a gelatin, about 1 hour.

Prepare the dough by mixing the flour and warm water. Knead until smooth. Cover and let the dough rest for about 30 minutes.

For the filling, mix together the ground pork, soy sauce, Shaoxing wine, sesame oil, sugar, white pepper, green onions, and grated ginger. Chop the set soup gelatin into small cubes and gently fold it into the pork filling.

Roll the dough into a long log and cut it into small pieces. Roll each piece into a thin, round wrapper about 3 inches in diameter.

Place a spoonful of the pork and gelatin mixture in the center of each wrapper. Carefully gather the edges and pleat to seal the dumplings, ensuring they are well closed.

To cook, line a steamer with cabbage leaves or parchment paper. Arrange the dumplings in the steamer, making sure they don't touch each other. Steam for about 10 minutes.

Serve the Xiao Long Bao immediately. Be cautious of the hot soup when biting into these delicious dumplings.

There you have it, Xiao Long Bao, a dish that's a true testament to the skill and flavors of Chinese culinary tradition. Enjoy the exquisite combination of tender dough, savory pork filling, and the delightful surprise of warm, flavorful soup in each dumpling. It's a culinary experience that's sure to impress.

Enjoy

86. Beef Broth & Onion Soup Dumplings

Today, we're making Beef Broth & Onion Soup Dumplings, a delightful twist on the traditional onion soup. These dumplings encapsulate the essence of the soup in a single bite, featuring a savory onion and beef filling encased in a soft, handcrafted dough.

Prep: 60 min. Cook: 30 min. Ready in: 1 h. 30 min. Servings: 4

Ingredients:

For the Dumpling Dough:
2 cups all-purpose flour
1/2 teaspoon salt
1/2 cup water
2 tablespoons olive oil

For the Filling:
2 tablespoons butter
2 large onions, thinly sliced
1 teaspoon sugar
1/2 teaspoon thyme
1/2 cup beef broth
Salt and pepper, to taste
1/2 cup grated Gruyère or Swiss cheese

For the Soup:
4 cups beef broth
1 bay leaf
1 teaspoon Worcestershire sauce
Salt and pepper, to taste

Cooking Directions:

Begin by preparing the dumpling dough. In a large mixing bowl, combine the flour and salt. Gradually add the water and olive oil, mixing to form a smooth dough. Knead the dough on a floured surface until it's soft and elastic. Let it rest for about 30 minutes.

For the filling, melt the butter in a pan over medium heat. Add the sliced onions and cook until caramelized, about 20 minutes. Stir in the sugar, thyme, and beef broth, and cook for an additional 10 minutes. Season with salt and pepper. Let the mixture cool, then mix in the grated cheese.

Roll out the dough on a floured surface. Cut it into small circles using a cookie cutter or a glass.

Place a spoonful of the onion and cheese filling onto each dough circle. Fold the dough over the filling to form a half-moon shape, pressing the edges to seal them tightly.

For the soup, bring the beef broth to a simmer in a pot. Add the bay leaf, Worcestershire sauce, salt, and pepper.

Carefully add the dumplings to the simmering broth. Cook for about 10 minutes, or until they float to the surface and the dough is cooked through.

Serve the Beef Broth & Onion Soup Dumplings hot, ensuring each bowl has a few dumplings and a generous amount of the flavorful broth.

Enjoy your Beef Broth & Onion Soup Dumplings, a dish that combines the warmth and comfort of onion soup with the joy of eating dumplings. Perfect for a chilly day or when you're in the mood for something hearty and satisfying, these dumplings offer a unique and delicious take on a classic soup.

Enjoy

87. Tomato Soup & Grilled Cheese Dumplings

Today, we're making Tomato Soup & Grilled Cheese Dumplings, a delightful twist on the beloved comfort food pairing. These dumplings encase the gooey, melted cheese and crispy bread of a grilled cheese sandwich, ready to be dipped into or served alongside a flavorful tomato soup.

Prep: 45 min. Cook: 20 min. Ready in: 1 h. 5 min. Servings: 4

Ingredients:

For the Dumplings:
2 cups all-purpose flour
1/2 teaspoon salt
1/2 cup water
2 tablespoons olive oil

For the Filling:
4 slices of bread, toasted
4 slices of cheddar cheese
Butter, for spreading

For the Tomato Soup:
2 tablespoons olive oil
1 small onion, chopped
2 cloves garlic, minced
1 can (14 oz) crushed tomatoes
2 cups vegetable broth
1 teaspoon sugar
Salt and pepper, to taste
1/2 teaspoon dried basil
1/4 cup heavy cream (optional for richness)

Cooking Directions:

Begin by preparing the dumpling dough. In a large mixing bowl, combine the flour and salt. Gradually add the water and olive oil, mixing to form a smooth dough. Knead the dough on a floured surface until it's soft and elastic. Let it rest for about 30 minutes.

For the filling, butter one side of each slice of toast and place a slice of cheddar cheese between two slices, buttered sides out, to make a sandwich. Cut the sandwiches into small pieces that will fit inside your dumplings.

Roll out the dough on a floured surface. Cut it into small circles using a cookie cutter or a glass.

Place a piece of the grilled cheese sandwich onto each dough circle. Fold the dough over the filling to form a half-moon shape, pressing the edges to seal them tightly.

For the tomato soup, heat olive oil in a pot over medium heat. Sauté the onion and garlic until soft. Add the crushed tomatoes, vegetable broth, sugar, salt, pepper, and dried basil. Simmer for about 20 minutes. Blend the soup until smooth, then stir in the heavy cream if using.

Heat a pot of water to a gentle boil. Cook the dumplings for about 10 minutes, or until they float to the surface and the dough is cooked through.

Serve the Tomato Soup & Grilled Cheese Dumplings hot, with the tomato soup on the side for dipping.

Enjoy your Tomato Soup & Grilled Cheese Dumplings, a dish that's sure to bring comfort and joy. This creative take on a classic pairing is perfect for a cozy meal, a playful appetizer, or whenever you're in the mood for something heartwarming and delicious.

Enjoy

88. Cold Peanut Noodle Dumplings

Today, we're making Cold Peanut Noodle Dumplings, a delightful dish that combines the nutty, savory flavors of peanut noodles with the fun and convenience of dumplings. This recipe is perfect for those who enjoy Asian flavors and are looking for a cold, refreshing dish.

Prep: 45 min. Cook: 15 min. Ready in: 1 h. Servings: 4

Ingredients:

For the Dumplings:

Store-bought or homemade dumpling wrappers

For the Peanut Noodle Filling:

1 cup cooked and cooled thin noodles (like soba or rice noodles)

1/4 cup creamy peanut butter

2 tablespoons soy sauce

1 tablespoon rice vinegar

1 teaspoon sesame oil

1 teaspoon honey

1 clove garlic, minced

1 teaspoon grated ginger

1/4 cup cucumber, finely chopped

1/4 cup carrot, finely chopped

2 tablespoons green onions, finely chopped

1 tablespoon cilantro, chopped

Crushed peanuts for garnish

Cooking Directions:

Begin by preparing the peanut noodle filling. In a large bowl, whisk together peanut butter, soy sauce, rice vinegar, sesame oil, honey, minced garlic, and grated ginger until smooth. Add the cooked noodles, cucumber, carrot, green onions, and cilantro. Toss everything together until the noodles are well coated with the sauce.

Lay out the dumpling wrappers on a clean surface. Place a spoonful of the peanut noodle mixture in the center of each wrapper.

Moisten the edges of the wrapper with water, fold it over the filling, and press to seal, forming a half-moon shape. Ensure the edges are tightly sealed.

Chill the dumplings in the refrigerator for about 30 minutes to set.

Serve the Cold Peanut Noodle Dumplings garnished with crushed peanuts. These dumplings are best enjoyed cold, offering a burst of rich and savory flavors with each bite.

Relish the unique and tasty experience of Cold Peanut Noodle Dumplings, a dish that's sure to be a hit, especially on hot summer days. Perfect for a light lunch, an appetizer, or a snack, these dumplings offer a delicious way to enjoy the flavors of peanut noodles in a novel and refreshing form.

Enjoy

89. Cold Cucumber & Dill Dumplings

Today, we're making Cold Cucumber & Dill Dumplings, a dish that's as delightful to the palate as it is to the eye. These dumplings are perfect for those who enjoy the light and crisp flavors of cucumber, enhanced with the subtle aroma of dill. They're ideal for a summer gathering or as a refreshing appetizer.

Prep: 30 min. Cook: 15 min. Ready in: 45 min. Servings: 4

Ingredients:

For the Dumplings:

Store-bought or homemade dumpling wrappers

For the Filling:

1 large cucumber, finely diced

2 tablespoons dill, freshly chopped

1 tablespoon lemon juice

1/2 teaspoon lemon zest

1/4 cup cream cheese, softened (use a dairy-free alternative for a vegan version)

Salt and pepper, to taste

1 clove garlic, minced

Cooking Directions:

Begin by preparing the filling. In a bowl, mix together the finely diced cucumber, chopped dill, lemon juice, lemon zest, and minced garlic. Add the softened cream cheese and season with salt and pepper. Stir until the mixture is well combined and creamy.

Lay out the dumpling wrappers on a clean surface. Place a small spoonful of the cucumber and dill mixture in the center of each wrapper.

Moisten the edges of the wrapper with water, fold it over the filling, and press to seal, forming a half-moon shape. Ensure the edges are tightly sealed.

Chill the dumplings in the refrigerator for about 15 minutes to allow the flavors to meld and the dumplings to firm up.

Serve the Cold Cucumber & Dill Dumplings as they are, offering a cool, crisp, and flavorful bite. You can accompany them with a light yogurt or sour cream-based dip if desired.

Enjoy your Cold Cucumber & Dill Dumplings, a refreshing and elegant dish that's sure to impress. These dumplings are a fantastic way to start a meal or to serve as part of a summer spread, offering a burst of fresh flavors in every bite.

Enjoy

90. Raw Vegan Fruit Dumplings

Today, we're making Raw Vegan Fruit Dumplings, a delightful and colorful dish that's as pleasing to the eye as it is to the palate. This recipe is perfect for those who love fruit and are looking for a creative and healthy way to enjoy it.

Prep: 30 min. Cook: 0 min. Ready in: 30 min. Servings: 4

Ingredients:

For the Dumpling Wrappers:

1 large mango, thinly sliced

Alternatively, use large papaya or pineapple slices

For the Fruit Filling:

1 cup strawberries, finely chopped

1 kiwi, peeled and finely chopped

1/2 cup blueberries, halved

1 banana, finely chopped

A drizzle of agave nectar or maple syrup

A squeeze of fresh lime juice

For Garnish:

Fresh mint leaves

A sprinkle of shredded coconut

Cooking Directions:

Begin by preparing the fruit wrappers. Use a sharp knife or a mandoline slicer to cut thin slices of mango. These slices will be used as the wrappers for your dumplings. If mango is not available, you can use papaya or pineapple as alternatives.

For the fruit filling, mix together the chopped strawberries, kiwi, blueberries, and banana in a bowl. Drizzle with agave nectar or maple syrup and add a squeeze of fresh lime juice. Gently mix to combine.

Place a spoonful of the fruit mixture onto each mango slice. Carefully fold the mango over the filling and roll it to encase the fruit mixture, similar to how you would roll a traditional dumpling or spring roll.

Chill the dumplings in the refrigerator for about 10 minutes to firm up slightly.

Serve the Raw Vegan Fruit Dumplings garnished with fresh mint leaves and a sprinkle of shredded coconut. Enjoy the burst of natural sweetness and freshness from these delightful fruit creations.

Savor the vibrant flavors and textures of your Raw Vegan Fruit Dumplings, a dish that's not only healthy but also a joy to eat. These dumplings are a perfect way to celebrate the natural sweetness and variety of fruits in a fun and creative form.

Enjoy

91. Raw Zucchini & Cashew Dumplings

Today, we're making Raw Zucchini & Cashew Dumplings, a refreshing and innovative dish that's perfect for a healthy snack or a creative starter. These dumplings are a wonderful blend of the subtle taste of zucchini and the rich, savory flavor of the cashew filling.

Prep: 45 min. Cook: None. Ready in: 45 min. Servings: 4

Ingredients:

For the Dumpling Wrappers:
2 large zucchinis, thinly sliced lengthwise (using a mandoline slicer for best results)

For the Cashew Filling:
1 cup raw cashews, soaked in water for 4 hours and drained
1 tablespoon nutritional yeast
1 clove garlic
Juice of 1 lemon
Salt and pepper, to taste
1/4 cup water, as needed for blending
2 tablespoons fresh herbs (like basil or parsley), finely chopped

For Garnish:
Fresh herbs (basil, parsley, or dill)
Red pepper flakes (optional)

Cooking Directions:

Begin by preparing the zucchini wrappers. Use a mandoline slicer to cut the zucchinis into thin, long slices. These will be used as the wrappers for your dumplings.

For the cashew filling, blend the soaked and drained cashews in a food processor with nutritional yeast, garlic, lemon juice, salt, and pepper. Add water as needed to achieve a smooth, creamy consistency. Transfer the mixture to a bowl and stir in the finely chopped herbs.

Place a spoonful of the cashew filling at one end of each zucchini slice. Carefully roll the zucchini around the filling, forming a dumpling shape.

Chill the dumplings in the refrigerator for about 15 minutes to firm up. Serve the Raw Zucchini & Cashew Dumplings garnished with fresh herbs and a sprinkle of red pepper flakes for a bit of heat, if desired. Enjoy the fresh, raw flavors and the creamy, nutty texture of the filling.

Relish the unique and delightful taste of your Raw Zucchini & Cashew Dumplings, a dish that's as nutritious as it is delicious. These dumplings are a fantastic way to enjoy the flavors of raw food in a creative and satisfying form, perfect for a light meal or a healthful snack.

Enjoy

92. Beet & Goat Cheese Dumplings

Today, we're making Beet & Goat Cheese Dumplings, a dish that's as delightful to look at as it is to taste. The vibrant color of the beet-infused dough paired with the rich flavor of the goat cheese filling makes these dumplings a true culinary delight.

Prep: 60 min. Cook: 20 min. Ready in: 1 h. 20 min. Servings: 4

Ingredients:

For the Dumpling Dough:

2 cups all-purpose flour

1/2 teaspoon salt

1/2 cup beet juice (for color and flavor)

Water, as needed

For the Filling:

1 cup goat cheese, softened

1/4 cup Parmesan cheese, grated

1 tablespoon fresh thyme, minced

Salt and pepper, to taste

1 small beet, roasted and finely diced

For Cooking:

Vegetable oil, for frying

Cooking Directions:

Begin by preparing the dumpling dough. In a large mixing bowl, combine the flour and salt. Gradually add the beet juice, mixing to form a smooth dough. Add water as needed to achieve the right consistency. Knead the dough on a floured surface until it's soft and elastic. Let it rest for about 30 minutes.

For the filling, in a bowl, mix together the goat cheese, Parmesan cheese, thyme, salt, and pepper. Gently fold in the roasted, diced beet.

Roll out the dough on a floured surface. Cut it into small circles using a cookie cutter or a glass.

Place a spoonful of the goat cheese and beet filling onto each dough circle. Fold the dough over the filling to form a half-moon shape, pressing the edges to seal them tightly.

Heat vegetable oil in a frying pan over medium heat. Fry the dumplings in batches until they are golden brown on both sides. Drain them on paper towels to remove excess oil.

Serve the Beet & Goat Cheese Dumplings hot. The combination of the sweet beet flavor with the tangy goat cheese creates a delightful and sophisticated dish that's sure to impress.

Savor the exquisite taste of your Beet & Goat Cheese Dumplings, a dish that perfectly combines visual appeal with flavorful sophistication. These dumplings are ideal for a special occasion or when you want to add a touch of elegance to your meal.

Enjoy

93. Pumpkin & Sage Dumplings

Today, we're making Pumpkin & Sage Dumplings, a dish that captures the essence of the fall season in every bite. The combination of pumpkin and sage in a soft, pillowy dumpling creates a delightful flavor experience that's both comforting and delicious.

Prep: 60 min. Cook: 20 min. Ready in: 1 h. 20 min. Servings: 4

Ingredients:

For the Dumpling Dough:

2 cups all-purpose flour

1/2 teaspoon salt

1/2 cup water

2 tablespoons olive oil

For the Filling:

1 cup pumpkin puree (canned or homemade)

1/4 cup Parmesan cheese, grated

1 tablespoon fresh sage, finely chopped

1/2 teaspoon nutmeg

Salt and pepper, to taste

For Cooking:

Butter, for frying

Additional fresh sage leaves for garnish

Cooking Directions:

Begin by preparing the dumpling dough. In a large mixing bowl, combine the flour and salt. Gradually add the water and olive oil, mixing to form a smooth dough. Knead the dough on a floured surface until it's soft and elastic. Let it rest for about 30 minutes.

For the filling, in a bowl, mix together the pumpkin puree, Parmesan cheese, chopped sage, nutmeg, salt, and pepper. The mixture should be smooth and well-seasoned.

Roll out the dough on a floured surface. Cut it into small circles using a cookie cutter or a glass.

Place a spoonful of the pumpkin filling onto each dough circle. Fold the dough over the filling to form a half-moon shape, pressing the edges to seal them tightly.

Heat a pan over medium heat and melt some butter. Fry the dumplings in batches until they are golden brown on both sides. Add additional butter as needed.

Serve the Pumpkin & Sage Dumplings hot, garnished with fresh sage leaves. These dumplings are a perfect way to celebrate the flavors of fall, offering a warm and hearty dish that's sure to comfort.

Enjoy your Pumpkin & Sage Dumplings, a dish that's as satisfying as it is flavorful. Whether you're enjoying a cozy night in or serving a special autumn-inspired meal, these dumplings are sure to be a hit with their blend of classic seasonal flavors.

Enjoy

94. Coffee & Cream Dumplings

Today, we're making Coffee & Cream Dumplings, a delightful dessert for those who can't get enough of coffee's deep and aromatic flavors. These dumplings offer a unique way to enjoy the beloved combination of coffee and cream in a sweet, doughy package.

Prep: 60 min. Cook: 20 min. Ready in: 1 h. 20 min. Servings: 4

Ingredients:

For the Dough:
2 cups all-purpose flour
1 tablespoon sugar
1/2 teaspoon salt
1/2 cup strong brewed coffee, cooled
2 tablespoons unsalted butter, melted

For the Filling:
1 cup mascarpone cheese
1/4 cup powdered sugar
1 teaspoon vanilla extract
2 tablespoons strong brewed coffee, cooled

For the Coffee Syrup:
1/2 cup strong brewed coffee
1/2 cup granulated sugar

Cooking Directions:

Begin by preparing the dough. In a large mixing bowl, combine the flour, sugar, and salt. Gradually add the cooled coffee and melted butter, mixing to form a smooth dough. Knead the dough on a floured surface until it's soft and elastic. Let it rest for about 30 minutes.

For the filling, in a bowl, mix together the mascarpone cheese, powdered sugar, vanilla extract, and cooled coffee. The mixture should be smooth and creamy.

Roll out the dough on a floured surface. Cut it into small circles using a cookie cutter or a glass.

Place a spoonful of the coffee cream filling onto each dough circle. Fold the dough over the filling to form a half-moon shape, pressing the edges to seal them tightly.

For the coffee syrup, in a small saucepan, combine the coffee and granulated sugar. Bring to a simmer over medium heat, stirring until the sugar dissolves. Reduce the heat and simmer until the mixture thickens into a syrup.

Cook the dumplings in a pot of boiling water for about 10 minutes, or until they float to the surface and are cooked through.

Serve the Coffee & Cream Dumplings warm, drizzled with the coffee syrup. Each bite will offer a harmonious blend of the rich coffee flavor with the sweet, creamy filling.

Indulge in the unique and delightful taste of your Coffee & Cream Dumplings, a dessert that's sure to impress with its inventive flavor profile. Perfect for coffee enthusiasts or as a sophisticated end to a meal, these dumplings provide a deliciously different dessert experience.

Enjoy

95. Pecan Pie Dumplings

Today, we're making Pecan Pie Dumplings, a delightful dessert that brings the beloved flavors of pecan pie into bite-sized treats. These dumplings are a perfect blend of sweet, nutty, and buttery tastes, making them an irresistible treat for any pecan pie lover.

Prep: 45 min. Cook: 20 min. Ready in: 1 h. 5 min. Servings: 4

Ingredients:

For the Dumplings:
Store-bought or homemade dumpling wrappers

For the Pecan Pie Filling:
1 cup pecans, chopped
1/2 cup brown sugar
1/4 cup maple syrup
2 tablespoons unsalted butter, melted
1 teaspoon vanilla extract
1/2 teaspoon cinnamon
A pinch of salt
1 egg, beaten (for binding)

For Serving:
Powdered sugar for dusting
Vanilla ice cream or whipped cream (optional)

Cooking Directions:

Begin by preparing the pecan pie filling. In a bowl, mix together the chopped pecans, brown sugar, maple syrup, melted butter, vanilla extract, cinnamon, and a pinch of salt. Add the beaten egg and mix until well combined.

Lay out the dumpling wrappers on a clean surface. Place a spoonful of the pecan pie filling in the center of each wrapper.

Moisten the edges of the wrapper with water, fold it over the filling, and press to seal, forming a half-moon shape. Ensure the edges are tightly sealed.

In a pot, bring water to a gentle boil. Cook the dumplings for about 10 minutes, or until they float to the surface and the wrapper is cooked through.

Serve the Pecan Pie Dumplings warm, dusted with powdered sugar. For added indulgence, serve with a scoop of vanilla ice cream or a dollop of whipped cream on the side.

Savor the deliciously sweet and nutty flavors of your Pecan Pie Dumplings, a dessert that's sure to be a hit with its unique twist on a classic pie. Whether enjoyed as a special treat or as part of a festive dessert spread, these dumplings offer a delightful and memorable taste experience.

Enjoy

96. Matcha & White Chocolate Dumplings

Today, we're making Matcha & White Chocolate Dumplings, a dessert that's as visually striking as it is delicious. These dumplings offer a harmonious blend of the distinctive taste of matcha with the rich, smooth flavor of white chocolate, creating a dessert that's both sophisticated and satisfying.

Prep: 45 min. Cook: 20 min. Ready in: 1 h. 5 min. Servings: 4

Ingredients:

For the Dumplings:

Store-bought or homemade dumpling wrappers

For the Filling:

1/2 cup white chocolate chips

2 tablespoons heavy cream

1 teaspoon matcha powder, plus extra for dusting

1/4 cup mascarpone cheese

For Serving:

Powdered sugar for dusting

Additional matcha powder

Cooking Directions:

Begin by preparing the filling. In a heatproof bowl, combine the white chocolate chips and heavy cream. Melt the mixture over a double boiler or in the microwave, stirring until smooth. Mix in the matcha powder and mascarpone cheese until well combined. Let the mixture cool and firm up slightly.

Lay out the dumpling wrappers on a clean surface. Place a spoonful of the matcha and white chocolate mixture in the center of each wrapper. Moisten the edges of the wrapper with water, fold it over the filling, and press to seal, forming a half-moon shape. Ensure the edges are tightly sealed.

Bring a pot of water to a gentle boil. Cook the dumplings for about 10 minutes, or until they float to the surface and the wrapper is cooked through.

Serve the Matcha & White Chocolate Dumplings warm or at room temperature, dusted with powdered sugar and additional matcha powder for an extra touch of flavor and color.

Indulge in the unique and exquisite flavors of your Matcha & White Chocolate Dumplings, a dessert that's sure to impress with its elegant taste and presentation. Perfect for tea lovers, dessert aficionados, or as a special treat, these dumplings are a delightful way to enjoy the fusion of Japanese and Western flavors.

Enjoy

97. Bourbon & Bacon Dumplings

Today, we're making Bourbon & Bacon Dumplings, a dish that's sure to be a hit with anyone who loves the combination of smoky, savory bacon and the rich flavor of bourbon. These dumplings are a fantastic choice for a unique appetizer or a bold snack.

Prep: 60 min. Cook: 20 min. Ready in: 1 h. 20 min. Servings: 4

Ingredients:

For the Dumplings:

Store-bought or homemade dumpling wrappers

For the Filling:

1/2 pound bacon, finely chopped

1 small onion, finely chopped

2 cloves garlic, minced

2 tablespoons bourbon

1 tablespoon brown sugar

Salt and pepper, to taste

1/4 cup cheddar cheese, grated (optional)

For Cooking:

Vegetable oil, for frying

Cooking Directions:

Begin by preparing the filling. In a pan, cook the bacon over medium heat until it's crispy. Remove the bacon and set it aside, leaving the bacon fat in the pan.

In the same pan, sauté the onion and garlic in the bacon fat until the onion is translucent. Add the bourbon and brown sugar, cooking for a few more minutes to allow the flavors to meld. Return the bacon to the pan, and season with salt and pepper. Remove from heat and let the mixture cool. If using, stir in the grated cheddar cheese.

Lay out the dumpling wrappers on a clean surface. Place a spoonful of the bacon and bourbon mixture in the center of each wrapper.

Moisten the edges of the wrapper with water, fold it over the filling, and press to seal, forming a half-moon shape. Ensure the edges are tightly sealed.

Heat vegetable oil in a frying pan over medium heat. Fry the dumplings in batches until they are golden brown on both sides. Drain them on paper towels to remove excess oil.

Serve the Bourbon & Bacon Dumplings hot. These dumplings offer a rich and satisfying flavor, with the smokiness of the bacon beautifully complemented by the sweet and warm notes of bourbon.

Enjoy your Bourbon & Bacon Dumplings, a dish that's as daring in flavor as it is satisfying. Perfect for an evening with friends, a special occasion, or when you're in the mood for something indulgently savory, these dumplings are sure to be a memorable treat.

Enjoy

98. Roasted Red Pepper & Feta Dumplings

Today, we're making Roasted Red Pepper & Feta Dumplings, a delightful dish that captures the essence of Mediterranean cuisine. The combination of sweet roasted peppers with salty feta and aromatic herbs makes these dumplings a fantastic option for a flavorful appetizer or a light meal.

Prep: 60 min. Cook: 20 min. Ready in: 1 h. 20 min. Servings: 4

Ingredients:

For the Dumplings:

Store-bought or homemade dumpling wrappers

For the Filling:

1 cup roasted red peppers, finely chopped

1 cup feta cheese, crumbled

1/4 cup Kalamata olives, pitted and chopped

1 tablespoon fresh basil, chopped

1 teaspoon dried oregano

Salt and pepper, to taste

For Cooking:

Olive oil, for frying

For Serving:

Tzatziki sauce or Greek yogurt for dipping

Cooking Directions:

Begin by preparing the filling. In a bowl, combine the finely chopped roasted red peppers, crumbled feta cheese, chopped Kalamata olives, fresh basil, and dried oregano. Season with salt and pepper, and mix well.

Lay out the dumpling wrappers on a clean surface. Place a spoonful of the roasted red pepper and feta mixture in the center of each wrapper. Moisten the edges of the wrapper with water, fold it over the filling, and press to seal, forming a half-moon shape. Ensure the edges are tightly sealed.

Heat olive oil in a frying pan over medium heat. Fry the dumplings in batches until they are golden brown on both sides. Drain them on paper towels to remove excess oil.

Serve the Roasted Red Pepper & Feta Dumplings hot, accompanied by tzatziki sauce or Greek yogurt for dipping. These dumplings offer a delightful burst of Mediterranean flavors, perfect for savoring on their own or as part of a larger spread.

Enjoy your Roasted Red Pepper & Feta Dumplings, a dish that brings a touch of the Mediterranean to your table. Whether you're hosting a dinner party, looking for a new appetizer idea, or simply in the mood for something different, these dumplings are sure to impress with their bright flavors and colorful presentation.

Enjoy

99. Wasabi & Tuna Dumplings

Today, we're making Wasabi & Tuna Dumplings, a dish that perfectly balances the freshness of tuna with the distinctive heat of wasabi. These dumplings are an excellent choice for a sophisticated appetizer or a light meal, especially for those who appreciate the flavors of Japanese cuisine.

Prep: 45 min. Cook: 15 min. Ready in: 60 min. Servings: 4

Ingredients:

For the Dumplings:

Store-bought or homemade dumpling wrappers

For the Filling:

1 cup sushi-grade tuna, finely chopped
1 tablespoon soy sauce
1 teaspoon sesame oil
1/2 teaspoon wasabi paste, or to taste
2 green onions, finely chopped
1 teaspoon black sesame seeds
Salt to taste

For Serving:

Soy sauce for dipping
Additional wasabi paste
Pickled ginger

Cooking Directions:

Begin by preparing the filling. In a bowl, mix together the finely chopped tuna, soy sauce, sesame oil, wasabi paste, green onions, and black sesame seeds. Season with salt and adjust the amount of wasabi according to your heat preference.

Lay out the dumpling wrappers on a clean surface. Place a spoonful of the wasabi tuna mixture in the center of each wrapper.

Moisten the edges of the wrapper with water, fold it over the filling, and press to seal, forming a half-moon shape. Ensure the edges are tightly sealed.

In a pot of boiling water, cook the dumplings for about 3 to 4 minutes, or until they float to the surface and are fully cooked. Alternatively, you can steam the dumplings if preferred.

Serve the Wasabi & Tuna Dumplings immediately, accompanied by soy sauce for dipping, additional wasabi paste, and pickled ginger on the side. These dumplings offer a refreshing and zesty flavor, perfect for enjoying with a cold drink or as part of a sushi dinner.

Savor the unique and exciting taste of your Wasabi & Tuna Dumplings, a dish that combines the best of the sea with the boldness of wasabi. Whether you're a sushi enthusiast or just looking for a new way to enjoy tuna, these dumplings are sure to delight your palate with their fresh and zesty flavors.

Enjoy

100. Popcorn Chicken Dumpling Pockets

Today, we're making Popcorn Chicken Dumpling Pockets, a dish that's sure to be a hit with both kids and adults alike. These dumpling pockets are filled with homemade crispy popcorn chicken, offering a delicious and satisfying bite every time.

Prep: 60 min. Cook: 30 min. Ready in: 1 h. 30 min. Servings: 4

Ingredients:

For the Dumpling Dough:

2 cups all-purpose flour

1/2 teaspoon salt

3/4 cup warm water

For the Popcorn Chicken:

1 pound boneless, skinless chicken thighs, cut into bite-sized pieces

1 cup buttermilk

1 cup all-purpose flour

1 teaspoon paprika

1 teaspoon garlic powder

Salt and pepper, to taste

Vegetable oil, for frying

For Assembly:

Your favorite dipping sauce (such as barbecue sauce, honey mustard, or ranch dressing)

Cooking Directions:

Begin by marinating the chicken. Place the chicken pieces in a bowl with the buttermilk and let them marinate for at least 30 minutes in the refrigerator.

Prepare the dumpling dough by mixing the flour and salt in a large bowl. Gradually add the warm water, mixing to form a smooth dough. Knead the dough on a floured surface until it's soft and elastic. Let it rest while you prepare the chicken.

In a separate bowl, combine the flour, paprika, garlic powder, salt, and pepper. Remove the chicken pieces from the buttermilk, then dredge them in the seasoned flour mixture.

Heat vegetable oil in a deep fryer or a large, deep pan to 375°F (190°C). Fry the chicken pieces in batches until golden brown and crispy, about 5 to 7 minutes. Drain on paper towels.

Roll out the dumpling dough on a floured surface and cut it into small squares.

Place a few pieces of popcorn chicken on each dough square. Fold the dough over the chicken to form a pocket, sealing the edges by pressing them together.

Steam the dumpling pockets in a steamer for about 10 minutes, or until the dough is cooked through.

Serve the Popcorn Chicken Dumpling Pockets hot, with your favorite dipping sauces on the side. These dumplings are perfect for a fun and casual meal or as a snack during game night or a movie.

Enjoy your Popcorn Chicken Dumpling Pockets, a creative and tasty dish that's perfect for any occasion. Whether you're looking for a new family favorite or a unique party snack, these dumpling pockets are sure to please everyone with their crispy, flavorful filling and soft, pillowy dough.

Enjoy

Bonus recipes for Dumpling dough

1. Basic Wheat Dumpling Dough
Ideal for: Meat and Vegetable Dumplings

Ingredients:
2 cups all-purpose flour
1/2 teaspoon salt
3/4 cup boiling water

Instructions:
In a large bowl, whisk together the flour and salt. Gradually add the boiling water, stirring with a fork until a shaggy dough forms. When cool enough to handle, knead on a floured surface until smooth. Cover with a damp cloth and rest for at least 30 minutes. This versatile dough has a neutral taste, making it suitable for a wide range of fillings.

2. Gluten-Free Dumpling Dough
Ideal for: Gluten-Free Prawn Har Gow and Gluten-Free Chicken & Herb Dumplings

Ingredients:
1 cup gluten-free all-purpose flour
1/4 cup tapioca starch
1/2 teaspoon xanthan gum (if not included in your flour blend)
1/2 teaspoon salt
1/2 cup warm water
1 tablespoon oil

Instructions:
Mix the gluten-free flour, tapioca starch, xanthan gum, and salt in a bowl. Add the warm water and oil, mixing to form a dough. Knead until smooth, adding more flour if the dough is too sticky. Let it rest, covered, for 30 minutes. This dough is designed to cater to those with gluten sensitivities without compromising on the dumpling's texture.

3. Rice Flour Dumpling Dough
Ideal for: Cold Peanut Noodle Dumplings and Cold Cucumber & Dill Dumplings

Ingredients:
2 cups rice flour
3/4 cup boiling water
1/4 teaspoon salt

Instructions:
Combine rice flour and salt in a large bowl. Slowly add the boiling water, stirring continuously until a dough starts to form. Knead gently until smooth. This dough is particularly sticky and delicate, perfect for lighter fillings and offers a slightly chewy texture when cooked.

4. Whole Wheat Dumpling Dough
Ideal for: Healthier, Fiber-rich Dumplings

Ingredients:
2 cups whole wheat flour
1/2 teaspoon salt
3/4 cup warm water

Instructions:
In a mixing bowl, combine the whole wheat flour and salt. Gradually add the warm water, mixing until a dough forms. Knead on a floured surface until elastic. Let it rest for 30 minutes. This dough brings a nutty flavor and more texture to dumplings, complementing robust fillings like beef or vegetables.

5. Spinach Dumpling Dough
Ideal for: Vibrant, Vegetable-packed Dumplings

Ingredients:
2 cups all-purpose flour
1/2 cup spinach puree (blend fresh spinach leaves with a bit of water)
1/2 teaspoon salt

Instructions:
Mix the flour and salt in a bowl. Add the spinach puree, mixing to incorporate. Knead until you achieve a smooth, elastic dough. Rest covered for at least 30 minutes. This dough adds a beautiful green color and subtle vegetable flavor, enhancing fillings with herbs or cheese.

Each dough recipe offers a unique base to complement various dumpling fillings, from traditional to innovative, ensuring every bite is as delightful as the flavors within.

Review Request

Thank you for purchasing Top 100 Most Delicious Dumpling Recipes.

We hope you found the recipes as tasteful and delicious as we do.

Please show your support and love for dumplings by leaving a review.

Make sure to check out all the other delicious recipes in the Top 100 Most Delicious cookbook series.

Printed in Great Britain
by Amazon